Praise for *Forward From Here*

"Ms. Lindbergh's famous, much-mythologized parents had many fascinating qualities, but they weren't known for big laughs. Charles and Anne Morrow Lindbergh's youngest child, however, has a comedian's timing. . . . Polygamy and other family matters are riotously chronicled in her new book and third memoir, *Forward From Here*, in which she writes about the view from age 60 and beyond, with one eyebrow firmly arched."
—Penelope Green, *The New York Times*

"In this collection of poignant essays, Lindbergh struggles to extract meaning, and even solace, from an imperfect everyday reality. . . . [Her] essays are suffused with a sly, gentle humor that supports her quiet resolve to carry on."
—*Publishers Weekly*

"[A] winsome meditation on aging and other matters. . . . Moving forward from here, whether as Gracious Old Lady or as Elderbabe, [Lindbergh] will surely be able to count on the largeness of heart and generosity of spirit that enrich her life, and the pages of this book."
—Judith Viorst, *The Washington Post Book World*

"Where does the time go? Not an original question, but one posed with a sweet mixture of humor and rue by Reeve Lindbergh. . . . From her mother, the poet Anne Morrow Lindbergh, she inherited her lyricism. From her father, the legendary aviator, she inherited a name to reckon with and a shocking legacy, having discovered a few years ago at the same time the world did that Charles Lindbergh secretly fathered families with three different women in Europe. She takes even this news generously in stride,

opening her heart to one more plot twist in the imponderable comedy of life."

—Amanda Heller, *The Boston Globe*

"Reeve Lindbergh is the youngest child of Charles and Anne Morrow Lindbergh and an author of warmth and wisdom. . . . Reading Lindbergh is like settling down in the kitchen with a cup of tea, to a chat with a very clear-eyed friend."

—Niki Nymark, *St. Louis Post-Dispatch*

FORWARD FROM HERE

Leaving Middle Age—and Other
Unexpected Adventures

Reeve Lindbergh

Simon & Schuster Paperbacks
NEW YORK   LONDON   TORONTO   SYDNEY

SIMON & SCHUSTER PAPERBACKS
A Division of Simon & Schuster, Inc.
1230 Avenue of the Americas
New York, NY 10020

First Simon & Schuster trade paperback edition April 2009

SIMON & SCHUSTER PAPERBACKS and colophon are registered
trademarks of Simon & Schuster, Inc.

For information about special discounts for bulk purchases,
please contact Simon & Schuster Special Sales at
1-800-456-6798 or business@simonandschuster.com.

Designed by Paul Dippolito

Manufactured in the United States of America

1   3   5   7   9   10   8   6   4   2

The Library of Congress has cataloged the hardcover as follows:

Lindbergh, Reeve.
Forward from here : leaving middle age and other unexpected
adventures / Reeve Lindbergh.
p.   cm.
Includes bibliographical references.
1. Older people—United States. 2. Aging—United States. I. Title
HQ1064.U5L556 2008
305.26'2—dc22   2007034483
ISBN-13: 978-0-7432-7511-8
ISBN-10:   0-7432-7511-X
ISBN-13: 978-0-7432-7512-5 (pbk)
ISBN-10:   0-7432-7512-8 (pbk)

To Nat

Contents

Contents

1. Hippies in the Hot Tub

When I first came to rural Vermont about thirty-five years ago, it was as an unknowing representative of a larger trend in my generation. This movement occurred just at the end of the Vietnam War and included several trajectories of philosophical and actual motion: from support of United States policies in Indochina to active opposition to the war; from traditional Western Judeo-Christian beliefs to Eastern spiritual practices, like Buddhism; from the stresses of American life in cities and suburbs to the slower pace of what has been called, erroneously, "the simple life" in places like Oregon, Montana, North Carolina, and northern New England.

Many of us were newlyweds or new partners and we arrived in pairs like the animals on Noah's ark. The optimists among us thought they were harbingers of a quieter, cleaner, saner way of life on the planet, returning to past customs in order to create a better future. The purists refused to use conventional electricity or plumbing. Instead they hauled water from brooks or springs, heated their homes exclusively with wood, and welcomed into their homes one or another of the many composting toilets available at the time, along with the colonies of fruit flies these devices inevitably bred.

Some native Vermonters, especially older ones who had spent their early years on farms without electricity or indoor plumbing and had been chopping, stacking, and burning firewood all their lives, smiled good-naturedly and shook their heads over the new-comers. To those kindhearted souls who befriended us and taught us what they could about country ways, we were just another generation of naive young people who would learn, as young people do, through time and experience.

Other, less charitable local citizens called us "hippie flat-landers." They did not smile as often, at us or at all. Those I still see around the area thirty-some-odd years later still don't smile much. I guess nobody ever taught them how.

Looking back over my journals from that time I am amused to see how quickly my own mood would swing between dismay and self-congratulation as I attempted to shape myself into a Country Woman. Here is a worried entry from October 16, 1971, about grocery shopping: "I am becoming <u>miserly</u>, I've noticed, comparing prices and saving money out loud . . ."

There is another soon afterward from the same period and on the same subject, only it sounds to me a little smug: "It's a new habit, this economy, like canning applesauce and baking bread. It gives me a purposeful self-image!"

I remember the ambivalence of those feelings. *I am being careful, I am being economical. I am pinching pennies, and this is necessary and good . . . I think . . . ?*

I know what that was all about. I was ambivalent because we were young then, and just starting out in family life, but we were not poor, not even close, and especially not compared to some of the people we had met in this area. I'd heard stories about very tough times, especially during the Depression, from an older neighbor couple, and I also had a local friend my own age, a horsewoman of some note, who was forced to sell a beloved prizewinning animal one winter to pay her bills.

There was some confusion in my mind as to whether too much obvious pinching of pennies on my part, since it was not absolutely necessary for me to do this, was insulting to my friends and my neighbors: patronizing, or pretentious, or just plain phony.

I thought that my "miserliness" might become a bad habit as well. It might be inconsistent with generosity of spirit, I thought. I thought an awful lot in those days.

I have learned since then, among other things, that poverty does not limit generosity; in fact the opposite may be true. It is an odd but interesting fact that in great human crises, poorer communities often give much more generously in proportion to their numbers than rich ones do. Of all the states in the Union listed in a recent survey measuring per capita generosity, it was Mississippi, one of the poorest in the nation, that came out on top in all three categories: tithing in church, tipping in restaurants, and contributions to charity. Maybe it takes real personal knowledge of need to make people reach out instinctively to help others.

Back in Vermont in the 1970s there was much to learn for young couples making the transition from an old way of life to a new one. The process may have been complicated, too, by the thought that we were doing exactly the reverse. We were "dropping out" of a modern world we did not admire and choosing to live in what we saw as a more old-fashioned context, imbued with the lost virtues of self-reliance, economy, and a healthy connection between the grower of food and the families it nourishes. We saw nothing but neighborliness along the country roads, nothing but a strong sense of community in the villages. We ignored the complaints of "small-mindedness" and "provincialism" we heard from a few local young people who were fleeing in the other direction, and we were not yet familiar with the long, insidious arm of small-town gossip.

At the same time that we were leaving urban areas to look for traditional values in the country, we were entering unknown territory in our own lives: beginning new partnerships, raising and caring for new babies and growing families, trying to make a living in a new place.

It was ironic that a village dating back to colonial times, a farmhouse built by a nineteenth-century farmer, or a home built beam by beam and board by board by a strong young couple from their own forest's trees, was each equally a "new" place for us, because we were living there for the first time. These were not necessarily "new" places for those people who had been born and raised in the area. The difference in perspective produced some interesting exchanges and gave rise to some unexpected relationships, as old-timers and newcomers became acquainted.

Most of the new people didn't know much about rural living, at first, which meant that the natives had many a good laugh over fancy city cars that skidded off icy roads in winter, or first-time home builders who put in the plumbing upside down and the wiring backward, and vice versa. On the other hand, local institutions and practices came in for their share of amusement and skepticism from displaced urbanites.

I saw several references by my writer contemporaries to the "toy-like" qualities of Vermont's small towns, each with its church, its general store, and its Town hall. One journalist, who must have been living with a preschool child at the time, referred to a Memorial Day parade as a "Fisher-Price" event, something that the toy company could have created, with its mayor, its firemen, its two or three veterans, and its tiny Boy Scout and Girl Scout troops.

This attitude did not play well locally. I remember coming into our village post office one day to find the postmistress in a rage. A woman who had just left the building, a well-known artist from a city far away, had offended her deeply by inquiring whether she had a "real" postal scale.

"This is a branch of the federal government!" the postmistress bristled. "Where does she think she is?"

For the most part, however, for old-timer and newcomer alike, it was a matter of living alongside each other day by day, over the months and the years. Unlikely alliances sprang up, first impressions gave way to second and third ones and sometimes even dissolved altogether as opinions changed, bonds were forged, and, occasionally, hearts were won.

There is something wonderful about unexpected affection, whether it develops between an octogenarian and an eight-year-old, a staunch conservative Republican and a progressive liberal Democrat, or a Yankee farmer and a hippie homesteader. It delights me that every so often the good feeling that two people have for each other is too strong for their biases and their upbringing, and defeats both in a flood of fellow feeling neither can explain. When this happens, there are sometimes wider repercussions in the community.

Friends of mine who came to Vermont in the 1970s arrived here from the academic world, with advanced degrees and plenty of energy, and started to build a log cabin in the woods. These two were smart and strong and very hardworking, so they didn't need a whole lot of help, but they did need some. There was a man living just down the road who was a very capable builder, and country-wise in many other ways, but he did not rate too highly in the opinions of his fellow townspeople.

According to another longtime local resident who spoke to me in strict confidence, this man belonged to a family considered disreputable for several generations. Everyone in town had been to school with him, or with his parents, or with his grandparents. His family's story was an old one. Everybody knew it, but nobody talked about it openly. This wasn't a matter of hatred or outright ostracism, it was just the way things were, the way things had always been. The common wisdom, informed by generations of shared experience, was that nobody in that family had ever amounted to very much, and it was more than likely that nobody in that family ever would.

My friends knew nothing about the town's history, or about local families and their reputations. When they met their neighbor for the first time they liked him and he liked them. They visited back and forth, and the young couple soon began to value the man's assistance. They developed a close friendship with him and with his family, one that continued throughout his life, and meant a great deal to all concerned.

I have always been both sentimental and idealistic, qualities that may not make me an objective interpreter of other peoples' experience. All the same, I could swear that the uncritical friendship of that young couple transformed this man's life. You could see it just in the way he began to carry himself and speak to other people and make his presence known around town. He seemed to be a different person, with new possibilities opening up before him. The people he knew, old-timers as well as newcomers, began to treat him differently. Something about the gift of a new perspective, from new people, had set him free.

I suspect this happened more than once in those days. Yes, some of us may have made the stupid mistake of looking at our new hometowns as if they were little toy villages containing little toy people and institutions, which was a diminishing and disrespectful point of view. On the other hand, some of us brought along another kind of stupidity, which seems to me a better one.

We had no social information, locally. We didn't have a clue as to who was the Respected Citizen and who was the Town Drunk. It was, in some cases, a liberating ignorance, not a bad thing for anybody.

There were a few stalwarts in what was then known as the Back-to-the-Land movement who did not want any help at all. My husband, Nat Tripp, who came to this part of Vermont not long after his time as a platoon leader in Vietnam, was one of these. He still tells stories about the work he and his first wife, Patty, undertook when they came here. They bought a farm at the end of an old dirt road, a place that had long since passed out of the hands of the original family and had sunk into disrepair.

I knew Nat and Patty back then. They were another new young couple in the area, the same age as my first husband, Richard, and I. They had both grown up in the same part of the world where I'd spent my own childhood, several hundred miles south of where the four of us now made our homes. He was a writer and she was an artist, whereas with Richard and me it was the other way around. We all got to be friends.

I remember that their labor seemed backbreaking and the hours they spent at it endless. Outside, they cleared daunting amounts of debris from around the house and barns, which were sadly dilapidated from years of neglect. Inside, there was just as much clearing to be done, and even more cleaning. The place was a mess, and even with the mellowing of my memory over the years, I know that is an understatement.

Nat had to do a good deal of construction after all the clearing and the cleaning, and some reconstruction, too. Some of the building was done right away to meet immediate needs, with their first child on the way and a Vermont winter approaching just as fast. Some of the work was done much more slowly, over the course of the years and the decades. It continued off and on throughout the life of that first marriage, a partnership that included its share of delights and difficulties, as did my own first marriage and as does any marriage, whatever its number.

The building work began all over again with another marriage, a second chance both for Nat and for me. We were middle-aged by then, and we were old friends when we joined forces. In some ways we were sadder and more seasoned than we had been when we first came to Vermont with our previous partners, but we were also full of a new joy, and a new eagerness to provide a good life for each other and for our now-mingled family.

The new construction started when I moved into Nat's home with my two teenage daughters in 1986. His sons, about the same age as my daughters, were here for the summers and on school holidays, and we were expecting a midlife baby, too. Nat was inspired to expand upon the work he and Patty had started when they lived in the house years ago and their two boys were small. He built new walls and installed new doors upstairs so that every teenager could have his or her own room when all four of our older children were in residence. Even our son, Ben, born the following spring, had a bedroom of his own. However small it might have to be, there was an indisputably private space for each child.

While remodeling and restoring the house for our expanding family, Nat often encountered the work of home repairmen of the past. He would pause now and then to think about his predecessors, he told me, those who had laid down the floorboards he was tearing up, those who had set the beams in place to form the walls for our children's rooms. There was a pleasant sense of fellowship in the work, as old and new were blended so that family life could continue on in the old farmhouse at the end of the road.

Once, though, while I was down in the kitchen, I heard him upstairs loudly swearing at something he had found in the course of his work.

"Who was the *idiot* who did this wiring?" he roared. I had no idea, so I kept quiet. There was a lot of fuming and fulminating overhead for a few minutes, and then there was silence. I waited, thinking I would soon hear more words or more work, one or the other. Instead, Nat himself came slowly and sheepishly down the stairs.

"It was me," he said. I don't know how he recognized his own long-ago handiwork, and I didn't ask. This house does for Nat what my old journals do for me. They remind him, sometimes forcefully, of his youth.

Our youth seems far behind us now, with most of our children now older than we were when we came to Vermont all those years ago, and with grandchildren (finally!) on the way. A number of the friends who were with us in the early years are still right here with us. One or two, sadly, have died, and some have gone on to other parts of the country and the world. It was a surprise to see that a few of the most eager hippie homesteaders did not last long in the country, but moved back to the cities they came from after a year or two. Others stayed, and combined small farming with careers much like those of our parents' generation: real estate, medicine, education, or the law. Wherever you choose to live, if you want to stay there you have to be able to make a living.

There are still some holdouts, though, people who are living off the land and off the grid, with homegrown vegetables and home-generated electricity and no television. More typical are the people who have found some happy compromise: the nurse practitioner who raises sheep and weaves beautiful rugs to sell; the hand knitter who markets her work over the Internet; the Buddhist lawyer, the doctor who plays chamber music, the minister who runs a roadside vegetable stand in summer with his family, and in his sermons as in his life addresses human ills from grief to global warming with what he calls "Episcopal Light and Power," a powerful not-for-profit noncorporation of good work and good-will.

Here we all are, then, thirty or forty years later, growing old gracefully or disgracefully, depending upon your point of view. We have our accretions of children and animals, our joys and our sorrows, our aches and our pains. We have our back-to-the-country principles, too, some intact and some in tatters, and some that can suddenly and painfully run up against the desire to age with comfort, if not with dignity, as the years go by.

Take, for instance, the issue of the hot tub.

Who ever heard of a hippie homesteader in a hot tub? What an image! Is this not the very antithesis of the ideals we lugged with us, fresh from Buckminster Fuller and Helen and Scott Nearing and a little less fresh from the nineteenth-century pen of that pond-dwelling tree hugger, Henry David Thoreau? What self-respecting urban-to-rural transplant after thirty-five years of life in Caledonia County in Vermont's Northeast Kingdom would even consider such a thing?

Well, me.

I have a recurring ache-and-pain in my right shoulder, and warm bubbly water, in moderation, helps a whole lot. I'd consider it. And I'm not alone, either. My husband the Vietnam veteran, who has a bad knee from jumping out of a helicopter thirty-five years ago or from a touch of arthritis right now, or both, would consider it, too. In fact, we have done more than consider it, we have gone out and purchased one, at a sale where it was called a "North Country Spa." We have not installed it yet, partly because we measured the thing incorrectly in the salesroom, and when it was delivered here we found that we could not get it through any of the doors.

The other thing that happened to us when the hot tub came was that we were overcome with a nostalgic miasma of moral confusion wafting back to us from the old days when we were all young, pain free, and inspired with a missionary zeal that some genius of the time called "born again rural."

Could we do this? Could we really bring ourselves to admit such an enormous and garish piece of luxury plumbing into our lives? Did our trifling twinges and ancient injuries really merit such self-indulgent, decadent behavior? Had we come down to this?

Never mind that even in the 1970s many hippies and home-steaders installed "saunas" or other hot tub equivalents in their homes just as soon as the walls were up. Never mind that many of our back-to-the-country friends from the old days were happily hot-tubbing it under their own roofs or under the stars right now. Never mind, either, that several of our native Vermont neighbors and friends were doing the same thing, those who had not already relocated to Florida. We were stricken with doubt, nonetheless, and with a sense of creeping geriatric turpitude.

What had happened to us? we asked ourselves. We weren't hot tub people! We were mountain stream people, we were Connecti-cut saltwater cove and Maine island tides people. If anything, con-sidering our geographic backgrounds, we should be *cold* tub people.

Nat hoisted the enormous, offensive white plastic package and its four-hundred-pound contents onto the loader of his tractor and tucked it away in the barn. Maybe we would try to return it to the spa store and get our money back (unlikely). Maybe we would give it to our niece, who owned a newly renovated but rarely inhabited home down the road (impractical). Maybe we would fill it with water from the barnyard pump in the springtime, and let the chickens swim in it (in their dreams!).

We felt saved, though embarrassed, knowing how very close we had come to giving in and sinking under and succumbing entirely to the siren song of the spa and the torpor of the tub, with its attendant pleasures: soothing oils; terry-cloth robes; those little yellow floating rubber ducks that are really thermometers. We closed the barn doors on all such nonsense, and returned to our perfectly happy, dry, and hot tub–less lives.

Then, because life is like that, something happened to change our perspective completely. Again. Actually, two things happened. First, Nat's oldest son announced that he and his wife were going to make us grandparents. Grandparents! One of our most cherished yearnings associated with the hot tub had to do with grandchildren splashing and chortling in it. A friend of mine has had a hot tub for twenty years, and describes her grandson, at the age of three and a half, coming to visit: "He left his shoes on the porch, his shirt in the kitchen, his pants in the dining room, and his underpants on the floor next to the hot tub." We had no grandchildren when we ordered ours, but we had still ordered the kind with a little shelf for their benefit and safety, should they ever make an appearance.

Another friend had already given us one of those thermometer rubber duckies early in our planning, but it was sitting in a cupboard unused and forgotten, its cheerful yellow body looking jaundiced and forlorn. Little did it know that its prospects were about to improve significantly, as soon as the second thing happened.

Nat measured the entrance to the woodshed. This is where he stacks the wood he cuts every year and brings in each fall for the two woodstoves and the fireplace in the living room. This woodshed is attached to the back of the house and has a big arched opening through which he can throw firewood from the truck to the woodshed floor. Then he stacks it in two piles, one on each side of the archway, in the area sheltered by the woodshed's walls. It is only a few steps across the woodshed floor to the door that opens onto our back hallway, and only a few steps down the hallway into our living room with its big open fireplace and its arm-chairs, its warm rug and its two comfortable sofas by the window.

I can see them already, with their little bare feet and their towels wrapped around their bodies, giggling and running down the hall. Grandchildren. Grandchildren love hot tubs, and we are going to have grandchildren. What could be more wonderful? They are too much for me, these little ghosts of both the future and of the past. They have overwhelmed my scruples and left them far behind me in the dust.

Nat measured the woodshed again, and measured the great white plastic package in the barn again, too. He got out the tractor and the loader, took the hot tub from the barn, and deposited it on the woodshed floor. We had by then picked up all the wood that was piled up one side of the woodshed and stacked it over on the other side, to make room. It fit perfectly.

Nat will put in the necessary electricity, something he knows how to do very well by now, and he'll figure out the plumbing, too. He certainly has all the experience and all the skills he needs for hot tub installation, after all these years on the farm. I've spent much of my life as a mother, a teacher, and a writer of children's books, in other words training to be a grandmother, so we're both all set.

So what happens if we are out in that woodshed someday, soaking and bubbling in that hot tub, and we are suddenly overcome with recollections of the days when we were younger and better people? I hope that we will simply lie back in the hot tub, and look fondly at each other, and enjoy the old memories along with the new ones.

And besides, as my husband suggested, "We can always pretend we're heating it with wood."

2. *Turtles*

On my husband's birthday, October 3, I saw wild geese flying overhead both morning and evening, and a turtle plodding manfully (or womanfully—it's hard to tell, with turtles) along our lane as I turned off the main road from town, heading toward our farm.

I was delighted, and stopped the car. A birthday turtle, for Nat! Nat loves turtles, and so do I. We have always hoped to have a lot of them in our new pond, which was dug for us with an excavator a couple of years ago, out behind the house and the orchard. Nat claims that it is not really a new pond, because a previous pond, or a body of water anyway, existed in that exact same spot in earlier times.

"What earlier times?" I asked, thinking of pioneer days: oxen standing knee-deep in the shallows, women in sunbonnets carrying water in wooden buckets. I was way, way off.

"In terms of anthropology it would be Neolithic, in terms of geology it would be the Holocene. About ten thousand years ago."

Another day, I saw what looked like an especially pretty painted turtle, so I got out of the car and walked over to it, and picked it up. The turtle didn't like this much. It drew in its head and waved its four delicate little turtle feet in the air in protest as I lifted it into the car. When I set it down on the seat next to me, the feet disappeared, too.

I looked reproachfully at the hole where the turtle's head had recently been. I told it that this was a *good* thing, being rescued from the road—I could so easily have been the UPS man, tearing along our lane to deliver a package. *Squish!* Turtle Doom.

The turtle didn't believe me, of course. When I got home and put it down on the kitchen floor for a minute, its head and limbs emerged again and it scrabbled around briefly looking for an exit, gathering dust in its tiny claws. I picked it up again, cleaned its feet by blowing on them, and put it in the big terrarium where our lizard, Ichabod, used to live. I put some hay from the barn in the terrarium so that the turtle's feet wouldn't slip on the glass floor, and I put some water in Ichabod's old dish, too, in case it got thirsty while I waited for Nat to come home.

This arrangement looked pretty comfortable to me, but the turtle was not satisfied. It rummaged around for quite a while, looking for a way to get out. After it came up against the glass walls a few times it got discouraged, pulled itself into its shell, and sat like a rock in one corner of the terrarium. This made me sad.

Nat was delighted with my discovery when he came home. "What a beauty!" he said admiringly, picking up the turtle gently and examining it. The turtle was still closed up inside its shell. I think it was pretending to be asleep. Together Nat and I walked out to the pond, where Nat put the animal gently down, right at the edge of the grassy bank.

Suddenly, the turtle woke up. It scrambled down the bank into the water, and as it went into the pond, it seemed to become another creature, slipping and sliding into its own element, then gliding away: soaring, graceful, free as any bird in the air.

At the end of October, I found another turtle, a much bigger one, at the edge of the River Road, which is a dirt road that goes along the Passumpsic River between the town of St. Johnsbury and the village of Passumpsic, just a couple of miles from our home.

This occurred during a period of warmer weather and rain that followed an autumn cold snap. In fact, it had been raining almost constantly for days now, so that the ground sank and squelched under my feet every time I crossed the lawn, and there was a burping, gurgling, roaring sound in the place where the little stream near our house runs underground. The noise echoed upward through the pipe that pokes out of the grass near this spot like a periscope on an interred submarine.

After passing the second turtle I once again slowed down, stopped the car, and got out. This time I wasn't immediately sure what I had seen: A rock? A toy? A strange escaped pet? When I walked back I could see at once that it was a snapping turtle. Even though I had not seen one before, snapping turtles are unmistakable. This animal was probably ten times the size of Nat's birthday turtle and as big around as a platter for a good-sized Thanksgiving turkey. Furthermore, it was not one bit pretty, except possibly in the eyes of another snapping turtle. It had a thick, ridged tail that reminded me of a Florida crocodile, and a scary-looking, almost prehistoric head, with a mouth like the beak of a very big, very bad bird.

The animal was doing nothing more ominous than lumbering along the residential side of the road, not the river side, and it had just crossed somebody's sandy driveway when I caught up to it. This was a much more formidable creature than the last turtle, I could tell. Still, I knew how happy the birthday turtle had made my husband, and I also vaguely remembered something he had told me, something that some Native American fishermen on the Hudson River had told him many years ago, about snapping turtles not biting if they were out of water. Or something like that. Anyway, I noticed that this turtle, as I studied its progress along the River Road, seemed quite slow and sleepy. Nat later suggested that the warmer weather, rain, and the resulting mud may have stirred this snapper from hibernation without awakening it fully.

This was probably fortunate. When I picked it up, one hand on either side of its massive shell, the turtle turned its head backward with a halfhearted, logy hiss and a snap of its beak, but this was not enough resistance to deter me. I put it in the back of my car and drove to the home of Ralph and Sue Bowen, our neighbors. The Bowens are both in their eighties, and Ralph had not been very well, so after speaking on the phone with Sue earlier in the day, I'd picked up a half gallon of milk for them at the store, before picking up the snapping turtle.

I gave Sue the milk, and then I opened the back of my vehicle to show her the turtle. It seemed a bit more animated now, with a quicker head movement and a louder hiss.

"Oh, my!" Sue said, endearing herself to me, not for the first time, by saying exactly what my mother would have said under the same circumstances.

By the time I arrived at my own house, I decided that it made sense to get a pair of gardening gloves. I put these on before picking up the turtle again, bringing it into the house, and depositing it in the downstairs bathroom, in the tub. Nobody was home at the time except for our dog, Elsa, and I had to leave again for a book program in Bradford, New Hampshire, so I closed the bathroom door and left a note on it for Nat and our son, Ben, since I knew they would return home before I did.

Oh, they were impressed! I called home after my program, on my cell phone, from White River Junction. I caught Nat just as he came into the house, and with the telephone in hand, he walked into the bathroom.

"Oh my God!" he said.

I was very pleased.

"Reevie, you've outdone yourself!" he exclaimed, and I knew what he meant. I'd out-turtled all previous turtles I'd ever found for him, anywhere, at any time.

I knew that, but I just wanted to hear it from him. I heard more, too.

"How did you pick him up?"

I told him, modestly. His voice changed.

"Reeve . . . They can lunge the full length of their bodies . . . Their necks are as long as their shells . . . They've been known to break broomsticks . . ."

He told me that the Native American fishermen on the Hudson had said snapping turtles don't bite "underwater," not "out of water," and besides, he thought they were maybe just baiting him . . . *Come on, white boy, take off all your clothes and swim with the snapping turtles . . .*

Nat was awed at what I had done. I did not choose to examine the implications of his awe.

I was smug. I had turtle magic. I was a turtle-whisperer.

When I got home, Nat and I together slid the turtle from the bathtub into a large canning kettle, very carefully, because it seemed the warmth of the house had woken the turtle up considerably. We took the kettle out and tipped it into the pond, and the snapping turtle disappeared, swimming gracefully into the depths like all the other turtles. I hope he's happy down there, and I hope he stays there.

That evening I heard Nat describing this adventure to a friend over the telephone, and I heard him say, ". . . Marilyn Monroe meets Godzilla!" He still sounded awed, even a little frightened. I hoped I was Marilyn.

3. Aging

The night before her eighth birthday, I found my daughter Lizzy weeping in her bed. "I love being seven," she sobbed, "I don't *want* to be eight!" I held her in my arms and explained at length that being eight was going to be even better than being seven. I told her how much I loved her and what a wonderful birthday she was going to have the next day. Eventually she was comforted, or maybe I just talked her to sleep.

I understood her feelings so well. It is always strange to imagine getting older, even when you aren't very old. I know that my own intense "When I Grow Up" yearnings throughout childhood were locked in combat with an equally intense wish that nothing would ever change. I never wanted to be a Grown-Up, or even an adolescent.

I don't remember whether I loved being seven, but I loved being twelve. At the very end of the year I was twelve years old I was afraid that I would become a different and detestable person on my thirteenth birthday. On that day, without my permission, I would wake up and not be a kid anymore. Instead I would be a Teenager. Instead of climbing trees and spending my days outdoors I would wear my hair in a perky ponytail, put on lipstick, and talk on the telephone constantly. I would grow breasts—these looked to me like a real nuisance at the time—and have to wear a Maiden-form bra with an uncomfortable elastic strap across my back. Obnoxious seventh-grade boys would see the strap through my shirt when they walked by me in the halls of the junior high school, and would reach out and "snap" it after I had passed. I'd seen this happen to other girls with my very own eyes. Worst of all, I could tell from the girls' responses to this annoying and cruel behavior that I would lose my senses and become brainlessly boy-crazy during this period. I *definitely* did not want to be thirteen.

When you are a child, every older child is significantly older, even if that child is only one grade ahead of you in school. Adults, of any age, are ancient. When I was twenty-four years old and teaching second grade in Readsboro, Vermont, one of my kindest students was a boy named Shawn, who asked me one day whether I had any children. After I'd confessed that I did not, he responded with sympathy: "What happened? Did they all grow up and leave home?"

In his eyes I was trembling on the brink of decrepitude with most of my life already over. I didn't see myself quite in that way, but I did already think I was pretty old, and I knew I was probably going to get even older. For some reason I thought this was a bad thing, and it took me a long time to change my mind. At twenty-six I felt perilously close to thirty. At thirty-nine I was not com-forted or inspired by Jack Benny's claim to be forever "thirty-nine and holding." At forty-five I wondered how I ever had arrived at such an age. All I ever asked was to be twelve! At fifty I blew out the candles with good humor, because I had to, but I gulped inside.

Ironically, much as I was afraid of aging from my childhood on, I was even more afraid of death. When I was very young I'd lie in bed at night and try to imagine what it was like to be dead. First I'd imagine myself in the ground, in a coffin, and I'd try to feel the weight of dirt packed in for a good six feet above me, with the green, well-mowed cemetery grass growing on top. I'd think about this until I could feel my heart beating faster and faster and had made myself so scared I wanted to throw up. What I was really imagining was being buried alive. I still can't think of anything much worse.

In less macabre moods I'd hope that death would be wiped out by the time I grew up, the way they had cured polio when I was in elementary school. Thanks to Jonas Salk I stood in line in the gymnasium of Hindley School to receive my polio shots with the other kids, everyone pretending together that we didn't care if it hurt. All of my friends were in line with me, and so was the boy from the other third grade who used to sock me in the stomach every so often for no reason I could understand. He'd just look at me and shoot his fist out *WHAM!* really fast into the area of my belly button and then out again so fast the teachers couldn't see. "He *likes* you, that's why," my friend said while I gasped and bent over, trying to feel flattered.

Probably they'd take care of death in a few years, I thought, right after polio. What would those shots feel like?

Fortunately, fears fed by the imagination tend to lose energy and diminish over time. Now I'm close to sixty, and though I don't always recognize the face I see in the mirror, something has changed in the way I think about aging and dying. I have an increased awareness of my own aging. The process increasingly interests and amazes me, annoys and irritates me, and sometimes it still frightens me, too, but much, much less than it used to. I find that along with the annoyance and irritation there is amusement—how often and in how many places can I lose my glasses in a day?—and that in the place of the old fear for my own physical survival there is an ongoing very real sadness at the absence of the friends and family members who have died before me.

It is remarkable to feel the strength of this emotion. After all the years of periodic anxiety about getting old, and about dying, I don't miss my youth even a tiny fraction as much as I miss my sister, Anne. Oh, how I wish that she were here, talking to me about age and death. She would make it seem so funny! She would complain eloquently and wittily about getting wrinkled and cranky and myopic. We would talk on the telephone every day about our bad memory and our sagging skin and our poor eyesight, the way we used to talk daily about our children and our dogs.

Anne died many years ago of cancer, though. I'm still here with the children, when they visit, since they all have grown up by now. There's a new set of dogs, and there are wrinkles and misplaced eyeglasses, too. I miss my sister as much as I did the day she died. I worry less and less, not more and more, about getting old myself. I don't mind if I do. I wish she could, too.

That's one reason why I don't have the same age-and-death dreads that I used to. There are other reasons, and I hope they all add up to maturity. (Or maybe it's just memory loss.) My concerns about life and death are more practical and less egocentric than they used to be, I hope. The other day while driving to see one of my daughters at a time when she felt stress and distress, I had to brake suddenly just at the end of the on-ramp of Interstate 91, to avoid a large truck that was speeding down from the north a lot faster than I'd anticipated. My first thought when the air cleared after the truck thundered past me was not for myself— *Thank God I'm alive!*—but for my daughter: *For heaven's sake, pay attention! All she needs this week is a dead mother!* This was a whole different emotional tone, more peevish but less selfish. Once I could breathe normally again, I decided I preferred it.

Driving habits may need increased vigilance, but the mellowness of feeling that comes with age makes life more pleasant, even for those who don't admit it. My husband came home from a meeting the other night surprised that he had had such a good time. He had spent most of the evening in conversation with someone he thought he didn't like. He and this man have very different political opinions, but they weren't talking about politics. They were talking about railroads, a mutually congenial topic. They are also a lot older than they were when they first met, and differed, years ago.

Nat told me that the man had "changed a lot." I asked how he thought this change had come about. He thought for a moment, then said, "Well, he's on the Atkins diet . . ."

I wonder what the other man said to his wife.

I don't know what further changes I will enjoy or endure as I age, but I do know the answer to the question I asked myself at thirty, and forty, and fifty: "How did I get to be this old?"

I was lucky.

Getting old is what I want to do. Getting old, whatever the years bring, is better by far than not getting old. Or, in the words of Maya Angelou, "Mostly, what I have learned so far about aging, despite the creakiness of one's bones and cragginess of one's once-silken skin, is this: do it. By all means, do it."

I am going to be sixty years old on my next birthday. This seems very old to me on some days. Then my friend Nardi Campion, almost ninety, writes about aging with the words "Oh, to be eighty-seven again!" and my thinking changes. If I can't be twelve years old forever, then when I grow up I want to be Nardi.

I watch myself preparing to turn sixty the way I prepared for turning thirty, and forty, and fifty. Watching myself, I perceive a certain amount of excited anticipation, the same feeling I get when the odometer on my car is at 999 miles and all its little inner workings are just about to turn and reveal "1000," that really important number represented by the numeral one and three zeros. *Before long,* I see myself thinking, *my numbers will turn and my age will be represented by the numeral six and a zero, a really important number.*

I'm also seeking guidance, but unobtrusively. Now I look at, but don't buy, the books in the bookstores that celebrate my next decade, with their cheerily whimsical titles, like *Now We Are Sixty* and *Suddenly Sixty*. Now I recall my mother saying, "Sixty is the youth of old age," when she was about seventy-five. Instead of rolling my eyes, the way I did when she actually said these things in my presence, I am grateful for the memory and I am relieved. Sixty is the *youth* of old age, I think. I'm just a child in this "aging" business. I can read the books, the way you read travel guides before a trip, but I don't have to enter the country. Not yet. That's good, because I'm not quite ready, though I'm getting there. I'm beginning to understand, at least, that this journey is inevitable and that it has been going on steadily for my whole life. I might as well enjoy the view as I travel along from my birth to death, inhabiting this being I call myself. I may be a passenger on the journey, or I may be the vehicle itself, but I'm definitely not the driver. I'm here, but I'm not in charge.

I used to see my life as an enormous self-improvement project, a work perpetually in progress. At any given time it was flawed, imperfect, awkward, and approximate, like the first draft of a manuscript, but I hoped there was plenty of time ahead for me to polish up the rough spots, revise, edit, and produce an acceptable final product. Someday, I thought, maybe I will be taller, more beautiful, more sophisticated, and less timid about things (cocktail parties, hornets, telephone calls to people I don't know). Someday maybe I will have read all of Henry James, and even some of William. Maybe I will have visited Greece, and Rome, and China. Maybe I will know, if not everything, much more than the little I know now. Maybe I will improve.

I never did get to be tall or gorgeous, William and Henry

remain incompletely read, I have yet to visit Greece, Rome, or China, I know more than I used to but a lot less than I hoped I would at this age. I have developed a kind of stamina for telephone calls and cocktail parties, but I'd still rather write a letter, on the one hand, or stay home and read, on the other. I may be a Grown-Up now, and a pretty old one at that, but I don't think I've improved as a human being since the time I was twelve. Whatever I was then, I am now, only older.

I have learned a few things over the years. I like the telephone a little better and I am braver about hornets, because children I have loved were more afraid of them than I was. Like my mother before me, I learned that if I saw a wasp crawling on my window I could locate a water glass and a stiff piece of cardboard, capture the dangerous insect, and put it outside a door or window, heroically protecting my family without hurting the creature. I do the same thing with spiders, not because I'm afraid of them but because I hate seeing them squished. Some people, when they see a spider, automatically reach out a big heavy foot and step on it—*squish*. Why do that? I'll never understand. A spider poses no danger to a human being, or at least not in my part of the world. Virtually any spider one encounters in daily life here is just going along minding its own business. Why kill it? The way some people can kill a small and living being without thinking makes me wonder whether the ability to take life easily is a matter of scale. I remember my father writing about the way a pilot flying a combat mission drops bombs that he can see only as tiny puffs of smoke when they land far below, while on the ground homes may be destroyed and families killed: mothers, fathers, babies, children, old people.

As I grew older and older, I got more used to the idea that death would happen to everybody, including me, but that in my case it would not happen for a very very very very long time. By the time it happened, I hoped, I would be so old that it wouldn't bother me. This is not quite true yet, but again, I think I may be getting there. I hope it takes me a while longer. There's no need to rush.

As I journey on, I carry my lost loved ones with me: my sister, my mother, and all the others. I have learned over the years that I can do this, that love continues beyond loss. It continues not abstractly but intimately, and it continues forever. My experience has also made me understand that loss is inevitable, and that loss, too, continues forever, right along with love.

Internally, quietly, always, I am awake to the possibilities of delight and of disaster. Delight is inherent in each instant, if one can take that perspective and hold it, gently, to heart. Delight is ever present and disaster may not ever come. But then again, it might. I know it is possible to drive around a corner in a quiet part of the world and come upon a terrible scene in which innocents have died. I know that it is possible to come home at the end of a normal, happy day and hear news so shocking and so painful that it will reverberate with hurt in the lives of people I love for many years to come. I know from experience, in fact, that "in the midst of life we are in death," as the Bible says. I am in the midst of my own life, or, by my calculations, about a quarter past midst, and there have been many deaths along the way, so I know that terrible things can happen to anyone, no matter what we have been told by our comforters, no matter what we may say to comfort our children.

What surprises and touches me is that I am still, all the same, prepared for delight. I can drive around a corner on a country road to witness, not a fatal accident, but a great blue heron rising up out of a lonely marsh into the evening sky. The slow ascent of its wings toward heaven matches a deep inhalation of my own breath, an expansion of my lungs and spirit into a place of rest and satisfaction.

I recently entered a building where a group of women in their eighties and nineties had gathered after a physical exercise program. These women carried canes, walked very slowly, and some of them moved with obvious difficulty down the stairs from the room where they had been working for an hour.

I was walking on emotional tiptoes as I approached them, thinking of my late mother and of the fading and falling away of her whole generation, those wonderful women who had survived two World Wars and the Depression. These women had made their way gallantly and with good manners through the turmoil of their century, and had led their daughters forward into another, better time for women. I thought of them with pride and gratitude, and with affection, and with sadness. Yes, they were passing on, I thought, this generation I loved. They were leaving me unprotected against the harsh winds of my own aging and my own dying to come. How would I manage without them? I walked past the group quietly, respectfully, wistfully.

But I was thrown off my tiptoes and solidly onto my feet again by a raucous burst of laughter. I turned to see three of these women in stitches, heads thrown back, laughing at something a fourth had said. Whatever it was had inspired an explosion of loud, unbridled merriment from these old ladies, and the noise filled the room. I laughed, too. I couldn't stop myself.

Everything happens in life. Some of what happens is terrible. We know this is true because it has always been true. But there is another truth available, an inexplicable and sometimes crazy truth that is no less compelling. The living of a life, day by day and moment by moment, is also wild with joy.

4. Ashes

Conversations with friends who are about my age are different now from the discussions we used to have thirty and forty years ago. In our twenties and thirties we talked about natural childbirth and breast-feeding, toilet training and preschools, teachers and extracurricular activities (the ski program; the ballet class; who is driving this week's car pool). In our sixties and seventies we sometimes find ourselves talking about long-term care insurance, environmentally sound retirement communities, living wills, end-of-life care, and ashes.

By now many of us have distributed the cremated remains of loved ones at least once, and those of us who have done so can't help thinking about the possible future disposition of our own cremated remains. I was told that these are known in the funeral home industry as "cremains," but the writer friend who heard this term at the same time I did protested, "It sounds like a French dessert!" And it does: *Crème de remains* . . . To use the word "cremains" makes me feel tacky and squeamish at the same time. I say ashes.

The discussion is always about the same thing: Where do you put them? People who die leaving instructions to have their bodies cremated don't always tell you what to do afterward. You have to figure it out.

If one strips away the somber clothing of grief and responsibility that accompanies such a task, it's a little like landscaping, home decorating, or planning a garden: delphiniums by the fence, sweet william along the border, Mother mixed in with the lilies of the valley. (This really was something my mother considered when she, in her time, was thinking about ashes. She was a lifelong gardener, and she said it would be so good for the lilies of the valley.)

There is quite a lot of choice these days, where ashes are concerned. You can have them interred in a small box in a cemetery plot along with the rest of the coffined relatives, you can have them scattered to the winds by airplane, or sent to the seas from a sailboat, or cast down a beautiful trout stream. You can have them dug into the soil in your garden or under the roots of a lovely old tree. The very wealthy can have their ashes launched into space now, I've heard, to orbit perpetually with the other debris out there. It costs a lot of money to be launched, but once you're there, there you are, going around and around in solitary splendor in your own chosen space-tomb, rather than orbiting with the rest of us who are living on, or buried in, the planet earth.

There is almost too much choice, I think. Sometimes people can't decide on just one resting place for the remains of a loved one, so they divide them up and scatter them in several places: in the garden of a childhood home; along a stretch of sand in some well-loved coastal area; by the grave of a spouse who passed on before; in a location near the home of a living partner or child.

My father was buried in Hawaii, but my mother's ashes were scattered in places she loved all over the world. (The lilies of the valley had to fend for themselves.) She left no instructions as to location, and it seemed right to her family that she should give herself to the earth as generously and as widely as she had done during her lifetime. Several of her children and grandchildren traveled with little boxes of ashes the year following her death.

They went to Switzerland, to Hawaii, to a special place on Florida's Gulf Coast, to Maine, to Vermont, and there was even a quiet canoe ride out into Long Island Sound, where two of us threw our mother's ashes to her favorite view. The mountains, the soil, and the sea all received her gently and in silence, as was fitting.

My sister's ashes went into Penobscot Bay, off a granite-pebbled, seaweed-strewn beach in North Haven, Maine. I suspect that the waters of Maine just off the islands in this bay have received the last remains of many family members from those who have lived or summered among these islands over the past century. Certainly my own family has become part of those waters again and again, our chalky dust and fine white ash floating off into a brisk east wind like so much chaff or thistledown, the tiny but heavier bits of bone falling the way pebbles do, onto the surface of the water and then through it, sinking and sifting down like salt or sand to obscurity below. There is sadness to this scattering, always, and there is a sense of uplifting freedom, too, but I'm never sure whose freedom it is. Theirs? Mine?

My mother-in-law, Alice Tripp, along with a younger sister and some friends, recently scattered her father's ashes off the town dock of a Maine island and into the waters of Penobscot Bay. My mother-in-law is now ninety-one, and her father has been dead for three decades. He sailed up and down the coast of Maine half a century ago. When fortune smiled on the family, he sailed a beautiful two-masted schooner whose photograph my husband still keeps on the wall of his office today. Later on, sadly, there were hard times and the schooner had to be sold. Sadder still, she went down in New England's legendary disaster, the hurricane of '38. The sailor, however, was undaunted. He built his own boat, a ketch a third the size of the ill-fated schooner, and went on sailing.

It may seem a long period between his passing and this final ceremony, but the man had seven daughters, all adults at the time of his death, most of them with families of their own. I assume that their intent was to perform this last service for their father at a moment when they could all be together. I suppose that the time was never quite right for such a reunion, and that the process was postponed again and again until it became one of those tasks that is put away and forgotten along with the ashes themselves, left sitting at the back of a shelf in some closet. This probably happens more often than people like to admit. (I've also heard of families not scattering a loved one's ashes at all, preferring to keep these at home in an urn on the mantelpiece, but I have never actually met anybody who did this.)

It was only after the sisters had grown older, in fact only after one or two of them had died, that the surviving daughters thought again of their original plan, and two of them finally carried it out.

I am sure that it was a very touching moment, with the sea and the sky all around them and the wind rippling the water of the harbor, gently rocking the sailboats of a new era, moored there by a new generation of sailors. It must have meant a lot to his daughters to return their father, finally, to the element he loved.

His grandsons have a slightly different perspective. My husband was one of them, and Nat actually sailed with his grandfather from time to time, as did some of his cousins. They all report that the deceased was a charming man but an absolutely terrible sailor. He went off course, he ran aground, he once snagged a telephone line with his mast. The grandsons say that the day his ashes were scattered from the town dock of the island was probably the only time their grandfather had made it into harbor without incident.

Disposition of ashes can become a thorny issue in a family. One widow complained to her children at the time her late, sedentary husband's ashes were taken to be scattered in a field by a beautiful river, "Your father *never* would have walked this far!"

One friend of mine had a terrible time finding a place to put her loved one's ashes, in spite of all the options. The difficulty was that the deceased had not been universally or even more than faintly loved by other people, with the exception of my friend. By the time she died, this woman had irritated or alienated just about everybody she had ever met. Nobody wanted this person's ashes planted in their garden, floating down their trout stream, scattered from their Maine beach, or resting under their lovely tree.

After much contemplation and a few false starts, my friend gave up on streams and gardens and trees and the coast of Maine. She made a reservation for lunch at a famous New York restaurant, one where the departed had dined often. My friend treated herself to a delicious meal and thought about her loved one while she ate it. She thought to herself how much the deceased would have enjoyed being with her and sharing the meal. Then she paid the bill, left a hefty tip, chose a moment when the waiter wasn't looking, and tipped the ashes into a potted palm.

"It was the one place where I knew she was always welcome," my friend explained.

It is good to have a loving friend and it is good to find the right place at the right time. May we all be so fortunate.

5. Time Flies

"Time flies," somebody said to me the other day, and I agreed with him automatically, but I'm still thinking about it. I was talking to Tony Adams of WCAX-TV in Burlington, Vermont, just before we taped an interview for his program, *Across the Fence*. We were discussing the strange feeling we both get when some young adult comes up and greets us enthusiastically, someone we know we should recognize but can't quite place in memory until the name is given:

"I'm Pete Williams!" Pete Williams, a child I knew long ago, now grown up.

"Oh, of course! Pete Williams! How nice to see you! How are you? What have you been doing since the last time we met?" What I really want to say is, *The last time we met you were "Petey Williams," and you were seven years old. How could you do this to me?*

It is always a shock to meet an adult shopping at the grocery store who used to be a shy second-grader in my classroom, or a member of a ballet class car pool when one of my daughters was in junior high school. But I stopped teaching second grade thirty-four years ago, and my dancing daughters have been through high school and college and have spent several years out in the working world. Why should I be surprised that their former classmates look like adults, as do my second-grade students from a time before my daughters were even born? I'm sure I don't look the way I did when these young adults knew me, either. In fact, I'm flattered that they even recognize me after all these years. Time flies.

Or does it? It seems just a minute ago I was a schoolteacher, but there was a time in my life, much earlier than that, when a summer of school vacation was as long and as full as a summer should be, and a school year, whether fourth grade or seventh, represented a whole era. In fourth grade I wore a long red scarf stuffed into the belt loops of my blue jeans, hoping to look like Burt Lancaster in *The Crimson Pirate*. My best friend was Alda Ament from next door, and I wanted wings—not the boring metal wings of airplanes but the real kind, with feathers. In seventh grade we wore "camel's hair" coats that had nothing to do with camels as far as I know, and clunky silver-plated ID bracelets. After you had your name engraved on your bracelet you could exchange it with your best friend, or with your boyfriend, if you had one.

There were teachers I looked up to in each epoch: Miss Taintor in fourth grade, Mr. Lyons and Miss Reed in seventh. There were special friendships all through those years: Alda Ament and Dorothy Moore, Wendy Barnum, Sue Field and Linda Ford. All of this set the tone of everyday life from September to early June. Then the school year dissolved into summer again, and the lazy stretch of days between June and the end of August was like a deep, cleansing breath that allowed everything to change completely, and a new era to begin in the fall: fifth grade with pretty Mrs. Forsberg, eighth grade and the binomial theorem in algebra II.

Time did not fly for me in eighth grade algebra class. Time crawled. I've never suffered with numbers so painfully, not even when the teacher's handbook instructed me to teach my second-graders that a "numeral" was the written symbol of a "number," but a "number" was an abstract mathematical concept. Try *that* on a seven-year-old who is only interested in wiggling a loose front tooth with her tongue until it falls out and she can put it under her pillow at night to collect a quarter from the tooth fairy the next morning. Twenty-five cents! At the time, that was a number (numeral?) with real meaning.

Time flies. Well, sometimes. I'm sure that a year in my classroom felt as long to my students as any elementary school year of my own did to me years earlier. But what about the later years, in middle school, high school, college, and beyond? Did time start flying then? Did the hours and the days move faster and faster until the seasons themselves were spinning in a wild circle of winterspringssummerfall, over and over? Is that what happens as we grow up?

No, I don't think so. Not for my students, or for me, or for any of us. It only seems that way when you look backward, and looking backward always distorts the view.

To find out what I was thinking at any time in my life, I can always reread my journal, but anybody who keeps one knows that journals don't give a complete picture, either. Journals are written consciously and selectively, whether they are the emotional outpourings of adolescents or the personal memoirs of monarchs. In a journal, any single entry reveals only one or two of the many experiences and thoughts the writer may have at a given moment. Still, each entry holds the immediacy of that particular chosen moment, with whatever it contained: a bird at the window, a child in a car, a voice on the telephone, an ache in the heart. By keeping a journal I can prevent myself, at least, from falsifying the truth of moments, which are real, which are present, which are *now*. When I read my old journals I can see the moments right there on the page, staring me in the face in my very own words.

When my daughters were very young and my son, Ben, had

not yet been born, I wrote about daily life in my journal, just as I do now. My journal entries as a mother of young children reflect a changing array of motherly moods: delight, exasperation, appreciation, exhaustion. In those days I was trying to be a wife and mother and a writer and a responsible member of my community: a Brownie troop leader, a Sunday school teacher, active in the parent-teacher group at the school. I also traveled for meetings of a nonprofit organization several times a year. The theme of my journals from those days was that I didn't "have enough time" for myself. Many of the entries were promises to "make more time" in the future:

I will try, at least, to make things a little bit better, somehow, step by step, year by year. It is better this year, but . . . it is very, very difficult, and heartbreakingly slow.

I wrote those words twenty-six years ago, in November. Yet the feeling I had as I read those lines last week was very familiar. I wondered, with sinking heart, whether I would find virtually the same complaint about not having enough of "my" time, and the promise to myself to "make more" of it, if I looked at my journal of this past November, a quarter of a century later. I was almost afraid to look but at the same time I was curious, so I did.

When I opened last year's journal a photograph fell out. It was an early ultrasound image of our very first, twin grandchildren, several months before their birth. I held I up to the light to look at the babies again, and was as amazed and as joyful as I had been when I saw this image for the first time. I tucked it away and started to read a November entry, written at Thanksgiving. It was mostly about brussels sprouts.

The holiday came just a few days after the death of Noel Perrin, our dear friend and brother-in-law, who was married to my sister, Anne, at the time of her own death in 1993. He shared Thanksgiving dinner with us for many years, except for the brussels sprouts.

Nat grows and cooks the tenderest, tastiest brussels sprouts I have ever eaten, and serves them every year with pride at the Thanksgiving holiday meal. Noel Perrin, whom we knew as Ned, loved most growing things and was a part-time farmer himself. He wrote essays about his agricultural adventures for magazines around the country, and published many of these in a series of books, the first of which was *First Person Rural*. He supported local farming with fervor, and one week a year he would eat only food grown within fifty miles of his home in Thetford, Vermont. Nonetheless, he hated brussels sprouts. He could not be persuaded to try even the brussels sprouts grown and cooked by his brother-in-law Nat, whose friendship he prized and whose culinary skills he praised far and wide. For many years, Ned would sit at the table politely as the brussels sprouts were passed from plate to plate, but he would not help himself even to one morsel. Nat teased him about it a little, as the rest of us helped ourselves to more of the deliciously prepared vegetable dish, and all of this became part of our holiday tradition. At last year's Thanksgiving dinner, with Ned absent from our table but present in our hearts, my husband could not bring himself to cook brussels sprouts at all.

I finished reading the Thanksgiving entry about Ned and the brussels sprouts, then I put the journal away. Last November, time was not flying. Time was delivering birth and death at its own measured tempo, lighting our lives and breaking our hearts and lighting our lives again, as it has done and as it will continue to do for as long as we ourselves are alive.

I looked back a few years earlier, though, and found a cantankerous little note to myself that seemed very apt. If time was not flying then, I was, and in far too many directions. I'd put myself into a nasty mood. Normally, I love working with small children and with fellow writers, I haunt bookstores and libraries, and a few months before this note was written I'd had a wonderful time at a party at the Smithsonian National Air and Space Museum, celebrating the seventy-fifth anniversary of my father's nonstop solo flight from New York to Paris in 1927. However, this memo, dated August 5, following what I remember as an unusually busy summer, has a snarling quality to it:

> *HEY REEVE!*
> *How about a !! VACATION!! for summer of 2003?*
> *(June–Aug) NO bookstores, NO libraries, No Little Kid*
> *stuff, NO "Lindy" stuff, NO Writers Conferences—*
> *NOTHING!—A little travel is permitted—And you can*
> *do a little writing, if all else fails. How About It?*
>
> *Love from REEVE*

Oh, dear. I can't say that my time-management skills have improved over the last quarter century, but I'm definitely getting crankier as I get older. I may be a little more conscious of who is responsible for all this excess activity, too.

There is a funny old-fashioned phrase, "What a to-do!" meaning "What a fuss!" or "What a commotion!" I think of it in terms of the way I so often have filled my life to the point of saturation with things I "have to do." I have to do this and I have to do that, and I *really* have to do the other thing, whether it's making a telephone call or folding the laundry or attending a meeting.

Some things need doing, it's true, and a healthy life for most people is a matter of movement and activity—doing things. Still, if

I'm not careful, all of my own personal "to-dos" will join forces, gather strength in numbers, and hover over my head like the cloud of dirt that travels with the Pig Pen character in the Charles Schulz cartoons. Without knowing how it happened, I'll find myself moving at the speed of a small and determined human tornado, driven by the fuss and commotion of what I am convinced I "have to do." What a to-do!

But why? Why do I have so much to do, and why do I have to do it in such a hurry? What am I hurrying to, or from? What do I think will happen if I slow down?

I don't deny that occupation brings life meaning along with livelihood, and I am well aware that a certain pace is set by the bearing and raising of children, just as a certain pace is maintained by the daily activities of the working world. But there is wisdom in what Alan Watts cautioned in his book *The Way of Zen:* "people in a hurry cannot feel." How often have I rushed into action, any action, in order to occupy and distract myself at a painful time? How often have I thought that "keeping busy" was the only way to meet any emotional challenge in life, from the anguish of grief to the confusion of divorce to the disorienting sense of having a home almost emptied of children after thirty-four years?

Time flies. A friend recently sent me a quote from the ecumenical religious scholar Donald Nicholl: "Hurry is a form of violence exercised upon time." I think this is true, and I believe that "killing time," were such a thing possible, truly would be a form of murder. At this point in my life I think of time as a living entity, a gift to each person born on earth and one we share with every creature alive with us on the planet at the same moment, from the newborn twins to the tree frogs around our pond.

Habitually busy, rushing, and hurried as I have been for so long, I wonder if I have the courage to go slower as I grow older, to become quieter, to go deeper, and to absorb and accept any feelings I may have, whatever they may be. I wonder whether I will learn to hurry less and to experience more, during the time I have left to be alive in the good company of all these other living things.

It amuses me now that I have so often thought of "my" time going too fast—time flies—or "heartbreakingly slow." Or too empty, or too full. What do I mean, "my time"? I have treated time as if it were a recalcitrant child, or a puppy that refuses to be house-trained: my personal property, my task, my grave responsibility. I seem to be both possessive of and possessed by time. I wonder if this same condition explains why people who can afford them wear very expensive watches. *Time is precious—so valuable that I keep it on my wrist, crusted with diamonds. Time is precious—and it's mine!*

Yes, I know that watches and clocks are the guardian angels of punctuality, and I don't mean to make fun of that virtue. Punctuality runs the world, but it is not universal. A Florida friend of mine was always late for appointments, and his meticulously prompt British assistant was finally provoked into asking him about a scheduled meeting, "Excuse me, but is that *your* eight o'clock, or *my* eight o'clock?"

In my grandmother Morrow's home there were two contradictory sentiments about time, each one represented by its own framed needlepoint phrase. The two hung side by side over a doorway. One of these came from my grandmother's lifelong friend Amey Aldrich, warning, "It is later than you think!" The other, reflecting the philosophy and character of my grandmother Elizabeth Morrow, or Grandma Bee, as we children referred to her, responded, "There is still time."

I take after my grandmother, alas, and too often think "there is

still time" when, in fact, there isn't. I find myself rushing franti-
cally to meetings and appointments in a state of anxiety and self-
criticism. *(Oh, no! What an idiot I am—late again!)*

It has occurred to me now and then that if I started out five
minutes earlier, just five minutes before I *think* I should leave the
house, I could travel in peace. I wonder if I am capable of giving
myself that five minutes, if I try. Or even ten minutes? How about
ten minutes? It wouldn't take more than just a little planning
every day to pick up the habit of leaving earlier. Couldn't I do
that?

A good friend of mine who has similar habits discovered one
day that she was always *exactly* ten minutes late to her appointments. She could set her watch by the consistency of her ten-
minutes-lateness. She became aware that she was not, as she had
thought, hopelessly, impossibly, and chaotically unpunctual. She
was instead meticulously and consistently and punctually unpunctual. She was astonished and cheered, and she set about to use this
new knowledge of herself to change her ways.

Maybe I can do the same thing. Maybe I can learn to give
myself a little extra time, so that I can see those cramped and hurried seconds blossoming into an expanded, hospitable bouquet of
moments. If I could do that, then rather than scurrying through
the day maybe I could bask and float a little, maybe I could rest
from all my rushing and become, in that sense anyway, a woman
of leisure. Time flies, but maybe I could learn to fly with rather
than against it.

I go back again and again to the poetry of Wallace Stevens. The
last three lines of his poem "Sunday Morning" have always especially appealed to me. I think it is because the words and the tone
together hold a suggestion of uncertainty and willingness in balance, traveling together in the direction of eventual grace:

At evening, casual flocks of pigeons make
Ambiguous undulations as they sink,
Downward to darkness, on extended wings

I appreciate the word "ambiguous" in the second line. It reminds me that I'm hoping not to sink "downward to darkness" today, or next week, or even next year. But the poet has offered something I find enormously comforting as I grow older: if time flies, and if I am willing to fly with it, then I can be airborne, too. I like that idea very much. After all, ever since I was in the fourth grade fifty years ago, I've wanted wings.

6. Birds and Boys

On the last day of January I saw a tree full of Bohemian Waxwings through a downstairs window. The tree was a small weeping crabapple that grows between the house and the garage, and the view from the window is always interesting. I once saw a moose through it, walking calmly between the two buildings, within twenty yards of where I stood watching, with only the window between us. It strolled along with a kind of nonchalant entitlement, as if a moose were no more out of place that near our house than a child on a bicycle.

This moose must have come up from the Andric Valley, where the Water Andric, or Andric Brook, so named by the early Scots who settled this area, marks the lower border of our farm. The animal seemed to be heading for higher ground and deeper woods at the top of our land, but not to be in any particular hurry about getting there. It walked by my window in a leisurely fashion, ambled up the hill, and disappeared from view.

As to the Bohemian Waxwings, I knew their proper name only because I had seen them on WCAX-TV, our Burlington television station, earlier that very morning. Our local weatherman said these birds were coming through the area in great flocks—I think he must have used the word "crowds" somewhere in the broadcast, because I heard the word "clouds." I was half listening, a cup of coffee in hand, and had to correct myself when I turned to see what he was talking about. Later, when the birds settled in the tree, I thought "clouds" seemed appropriate: clouds of Bohemian Waxwings, with light-golden bodies and little ruffs on their heads. They looked to me like Blonde Bombshell Blue Jays, our northern raucous jay's cute cousins just in from Southern California.

Bohemian Waxwings have black masks, too, and little brownish red rumps, or whatever the official name is for the area under the tail that would be called the "stern" if the bird were a boat. Best of all, they have bright orange-yellow wing bars, and their wings are always moving. The first impression you get when a group of them appears is of a sudden influx of movement and light. It's as if a host of very small angels has arrived.

I was very taken with this bunch. I watched them off and on all day. They would fly from a very high vantage point at the top of the two big maples on the far side of the house, where the hammock hangs in summer, right over the roof of the house to the low, wide-branched wild crabapple tree on the other side, where I first saw them. Then they would fly back again. They did this hundreds of times. After a while I found myself wanting to know more about these creatures whose wings were beating so intensely over my head and over my house. I went to look for what I call "the bird book," more commonly known as *A Field Guide to the Birds,* by Roger Tory Peterson, but I could not find it anywhere.

Nat was away for a few days at the time, and I didn't think I should track him down to ask where the bird book was. I should be able to find it myself. I went upstairs and looked in the bookcase where I thought it should be. That's what I do when I lose something: I look for it where I think it should be, the place I think of as its rightful home.

Most often the thing I am looking for is not there, but if I ever do find it, that's where I return it, hoping to be right the next time. During all the time before I do that, the time I spend *not* finding it, I grumble about how it should be in that place, and why isn't it there, and who took it away to put somewhere else, anyway?

I looked in the bookcase at the top of the back stairs, the bookcase that runs between the room that used to be my daughter Lizzy's when she lived here about fifteen years ago, and the room that used to be her younger sister Susannah's. Two of the other bedrooms on the second floor once belonged to our sons Eli and Sam; one is still inhabited by our son Ben, who will leave home in June. This bookcase is just across from Eli's and Sam's rooms. They were here with Lizzy and Susannah and us during summers and holidays in that same period. It stands just to the left of Ben's room.

There were a lot of empty rooms around me, I noticed while I was looking unsuccessfully for the bird book. I felt an old, familiar pang. I knew what it was, and I knew I should be much, much too mature and serene to feel it at my time of life. Four of the five children who once lived in these rooms are well into their twenties, and a couple of them are in their thirties. They all have loving partners and homes of their own. In one case, delightfully, there are babies on the way. They all return to visit us, every year, even though they don't live here anymore.

This is all wonderful, but I still noticed the empty rooms, and I still felt the pang. It was as strong as it has ever been, in fact it was stronger, to be truthful. Ben is our last child, and younger than the youngest of his older siblings by almost a decade. I know we will enjoy watching him spread his wings and soar off into the fullness of adulthood, just as the others did. All the same, there is something about knowing that it will actually happen, not in a few years but in a few months, and for the very last time in my life, that really hurts. And yet I wouldn't want it to be any other way.

And knowing this to be true, it still really hurts, which makes no sense. And I am sure I am not the only parent who feels exactly this same way.

I am anticipating the final emptying of my nest with real sadness, along with what seems to me an irrational kind of bewilderment. After so many years with children growing up in my home and then going out into the world, I have gotten to know this process very well, and learned to appreciate it fully every time it happens. Nonetheless, I have trouble with myself when it is going on. At the moment that my children are actually preparing to leave home, "in real time," as the saying goes, I have difficulty maintaining the delicate balance of connection and disconnection that I know so well, a balance that is critical to the dance of parent and child. It must be practiced with great care and increasing skill over the years, in order to tread the long, lovely measures of parenthood with sustaining and necessary grace.

Someone once said that if you are a parent, your job is to work just as hard as you can for many years toward the goal of putting yourself out of a job. There is some truth to this notion, though it is also true that anyone who has ever been a parent will always be one, just as anyone who was ever born will always be someone's daughter or son, someone's sister or brother, someone's grandchild, cousin, nephew, niece. We owe our very existence to a web of close family relationships, and we live within them whether we choose to acknowledge this or not. We are connected to one another from birth to death as inevitably as any flock of birds.

Where was the bird book? Every other field guide imaginable was in the bookcase: *A Field Guide to the Ferns; A Field Guide to Butterflies; A Field Guide to North American Weather; A Field Guide to Edible Plants; A Field Guide to Shells; A Field Guide to Reptiles and Amphibians.* No, this was not turtle season. What I needed was the bird book, and I just could not find it, anywhere. Finally, after a frustrating search, including a certain amount of circling back and glaring at the bookcase where the bird book should have been but wasn't, I gave up.

Oh, well, I thought. I had the birds themselves, didn't I? Why did I need the bird book? The birds don't have one, for heaven's sake. They don't even know their names. "Bohemian Waxwing" is merely a descriptive phrase invented by pitiful featherless observers like John James Audubon and Mr. Peterson, for the benefit of even more pitiful featherless observers like me, creatures who can neither flap nor flutter. The words in the *Field Guide to the Birds* had no real relationship to these winged beings outside my window. They were guided only by the forces of season and climate and food supply, driven on by the urge to feed and breed in order to replace themselves with another generation in what is, if you think about it, a frighteningly short period. Who has time for bird books? Not birds, that's for sure.

The one drawback to all the feathery magic of that day was that the flock of birds, flying back and forth over the house from one side to the other, left a remarkable amount of Bohemian Waxwing poop on the windshield of my car, which I had parked foolishly close to the maple trees and directly under those high branches where the birds, intermittently, perched.

Even one bird's droppings coming from that height would have made a mighty splat on a windshield, and there must have been between fifty and a hundred birds. I knew I would have a lot of work to do before I could use the car the next morning, but I didn't care. I sat at my desk upstairs working all the afternoon, and I watched them first swoop over from the maple trees, then settle in the crabapple tree to eat crabapples for a while, then flash their bright wings and rise up like sunlit dust in the wind or like a flurry of gold snowflakes, and disappear over the house again. I watched until it grew dark, and still the birds were flying.

In the morning the crabapple tree was completely bare and the birds were gone. I found the bird book, though. It was on the mantelpiece in the living room, under the big box of matches we use for the fireplace, with the binoculars. Of course. My husband told me where to look for it when he called from Miami in the evening. He said that the Bohemian Waxwings come through every year, stopping only long enough to strip the crabapple tree of every last apple before they move on. He was delighted to know that they had paid me a visit in his absence. (I refrained from pointing out that his truck, unlike my car, was parked under cover at the Burlington airport at the time, splat-free.)

In our home the bird book is Roger Tory Peterson's *A Field Guide to the Birds, Second Revised and Enlarged Edition*. (Sponsored by National Audubon Society, published by Houghton Mifflin Company, Boston, 1947.)

After all the fuss I made about finding the book, I decided when I read the description of Bohemian Waxwings that the bird book really does not do these birds justice. The picture (Pl. 46) is sedate and bland, and the identifying caption opposite gives no hint of the golden motion I watched all afternoon. It says only, "White wing-patches, rusty under tail-coverts." I never would have remembered the words "tail-coverts." As for the description (p. 130), well, here it is:

WAXWINGS Bombycillidae

BOHEMIAN WAXWING *Bombycilla garrulus pallidiceps* Pl. 46

Similar species: $7\frac{1}{2} - 8\frac{1}{2}$. Resembles the Cedar Waxwing closely, but is larger, has some *white in the wing*, is grayer, and has *chestnut-red* under tail-coverts instead of white.

Voice: A low *zreee*, rougher than note of Cedar Waxwing.

Range: Breeds in w. Canada; winters irregularly to n.-cent. States and rarely to ne. states.

I closed the book again, more disappointed than inspired by the information it offered. I decided that I was better off remaining ignorant of the facts, dazzled by my own one-day's vision of wings and light.

About a week later, Ben came home one evening with a group of friends. Many of these were classmates he'd known since kindergarten, children I had seen at the house many times before, individually or in groups, for birthday parties and overnights and after-school gatherings for years. He had asked if he could bring "some friends over," and we had agreed, but there were ten of them, and when they came into the house it seemed like a large crowd. They were all as friendly and polite as they could be, but they were so *big,* all of a sudden, compared to all of their previous sizes going back through the years. They went outside together in the snow, dragging sleds and toboggans high up to the top of the hill and sliding or tumbling down again, their shouts and laughter echoing throughout the farm's winter landscape. When they came in again they were wet and hungry. They spent a couple of hours drying off and playing cards in the living room, the house strewn with parkas, hats, boots, mittens, scarves, and the occasional sodden sock.

They ate the following:

1 box of Triscuits
1½ pounds of Jarlsberg cheese
6 packages of ramen noodle soup
1 entire roast chicken
2 packages frozen peas
2 boxes of red beans and rice (cooked)

They also polished off a half gallon of milk and a half gallon of orange juice.

I thought I had better do something, so I made a quick trip to the grocery store. I bought a whole gallon each of milk and orange juice and a gallon of cranberry-raspberry juice as well. I bought two packages of English muffins and two packages of the kind of waffles you can put in the toaster. I got a pound of butter, two packages of ready-to-bake cinnamon rolls, and three boxes of assorted cereals. I thought maybe everybody would be spending the night.

When I arrived home with all the groceries, there were no cars in the driveway except for my own, and Nat's truck. When I entered the house it was quiet. All of the children were gone. Nat told me that Ben would be back later with one friend who would stay overnight, most likely in Sam's old room. They all had gone to the dance at the school, but the others would go on to their own homes afterward.

I knew how the parents would feel when their children got home safely at the end of the evening, and I knew how the parents would feel when their children went to school the next morning. I know how the parents will feel, too, when their children leave home, as mine will, in the fall.

I put away the groceries without complaint because I was well aware that everything would get eaten sooner or later. Then, all of a sudden, I thought of the Bohemian Waxwings. They came suddenly a glorious golden visitation in my life, for a short but very important period of time in their own lives. They made a mess, they ate everything in sight, and then they were gone.

They'll be back, I said to myself as I put away the cranberry-raspberry juice on the bottom shelf of the refrigerator. They always come back, after all. I know that. And when they do. I'll be ready for them.

7. Gift from Captiva

February 22, 2004 *Morning of the First Day*

I am in Florida for a few days, staying by myself on the island of Captiva, not far from the little house on the beach, now long gone, where my mother lived while writing her 1955 book, *Gift from the Sea,* almost fifty years ago.

I read this book at least once a year, and I always read it again when I am in Florida. This is the first time I have ever read it while staying alone on Captiva.

This island was a very different place when my mother was here in the 1950s. There was a small local population, little tourism or real estate development, and above all, no causeway from the mainland to bring the automobiles and vacationing families of today.

I'm staying here this week in a small, single-story, white-painted cottage that is part of the Captiva Island Inn on Andy Rosse Lane. There are shops and restaurants all around me, and people and cars everywhere. There are also lush palm trees, tall pines, bushes of blooming hibiscus, and cascades of bright pink bougainvillea. I am surrounded by the wings and songs of birds I see in New England only in the summer, or not at all, and it is an easy walk to the beach in the morning.

I would love to have spent a week here fifty years ago. I would be glad if there were no long lines of traffic in South Florida (or anywhere else in the world, for that matter). I like thinking today about the privacy and quietness my mother knew here.

Still, whatever I think I might have loved in another era, I am here now. I live in this moment, along with all the other creatures living on the planet with me. Like the snowy egret that sits in the palm tree just over the café across the street, like the great blue heron that stands at the edge of the tide, like the mynah birds squeaking and darting in the bushes by the restaurant where I get my breakfast, I belong to my own time.

I take a walk on the beach before I settle down to work in the mornings. The very first thing I see, the first day as I come out onto the sand from the pine-needle path between road and shore, is a collection of large, brightly colored "WaveRunner" Jet Skis, lined up in the sunshine on a sand dune. A score of life preservers hangs from a pole nearby, but there are few people.

One or two families have settled under beach umbrellas along the shore. At the shoreline itself, the waves are almost turquoise and they come in gently, one following the other in the even, end-less hiss and roar and give and take of tidal movement. This is so much like a kind of respiration that I have actually slowed down my breathing here, keeping time to the quiet rhythm of the Gulf of Mexico.

Two great blue herons stand, impassive as sentries, on either side of a fifty-yard section of beach umbrellas. One of these birds has its back to the surf, the other is facing the sea, standing within a dozen feet of a man fishing. The man does not look as if he belongs with the families under the umbrellas. He is wearing a white T-shirt and navy Bermuda shorts, and he appears to be in his seventies. He holds a fishing rod with its line dropped into the waves quite near the shore, and there is a galvanized bucket a little higher up on the sand behind him, awaiting his catch.

Suddenly I see a flash of silver, and the fisherman reels in a fish. It is not very big. This is not a Hemingwayesque "Old Man and the Sea" moment of triumph. This is an elderly man with a small fish. In a moment, he takes his catch off the hook. I expect him to turn next toward the bucket on the sand. Instead, he lets his arm drop, with the fish still in his hand, and then he throws it into the air sideways. There is another flash, a quick arc of motion and light in the direction of the heron at his side. The bird opens its beak, the fish tail flicks once and disappears into the wide scissor-wedge—gulp—gone.

A laughing child runs down the beach toward the water. The heron sidesteps away from this small commotion but soon steps back again and holds its ground, waiting. Neither bird nor fisherman pays any attention to me at all. I walk on.

What will I find on this beach, I wonder, walking along the sand so long after my mother did? Another woman in another era, my mother has died, and somehow I feel sure I will not find the shells she found, the ones for which she named five of her chapters. Each shell she wrote about reflected some aspect of her thought.

The channeled whelk represented "the ideal of a simplified life"; the moon shell reminded her of that great, neglected treasure in human experience, solitude. The fragile double-sunrise bivalve recalled the fleeting but nonetheless beautiful "one-and-only" moments of romantic love, and the homely, familiar oyster shell spoke to her of marriage and family life, with all its "burdens and excrescences," its lumps and its bumps and its awkward functionality.

Finally, there was the argonauta, the paper nautilus, whose resident maternal creature used her shell, my mother wrote, as "a cradle for the young, held in the arms of the mother Argonaut who floats with it to the surface, where the eggs hatch and the young swim away. Then the mother Argonaut leaves her shell and starts another life." I always think about this chapter for a long time after I have read it. I'm sure I won't find an argonauta on this beach.

I do find a plastic drinking cup somebody thoughtlessly threw away, and resolve that I will take it back to my room and dispose of it. Meanwhile it is handy for collecting beach treasures.

The first channeled whelk I find is broken. I pick it up and eye it sadly, a damaged and diminished thing resting in the palm of my hand. I look once again, just before dropping it on the sand, but this time, for some reason, I can really see what I'm looking at.

Sometimes this happens to me, if I'm lucky. I get a moment when I can see the world in freshness, the way children do. I can see with my eyes, that is, without the weight and confusion of my ideas and my conclusions rushing in at the same time: *Oh, dear, a broken shell, so damaged and useless, it's too bad and it's so sad. Nothing stays the same, the world of today is so much worse than it used to be fifty years ago, and it is deteriorating every minute, even as I think these thoughts—how awful.*

I look and I see. This is a lovely object! What was I thinking? This is not simply a broken whelk, but also a tiny, beautiful piece of sculpture, its shape as classic and graceful as any three-dimensional work of art I've ever seen. Imperfect as the shell is, the sea has worn smooth the imperfections. Now the core spiral is exposed intact, and what is left of the outer curve of shell reaches over it, protective in suggestion if not in actual presence. The eye wants to look further inside, and the hand to form a cradle around the spiraling turns.

I find myself thinking not of *Gift from the Sea,* but of the last verse of my mother's poem "Broken Shell," in another book entirely, her 1956 collection, *The Unicorn and Other Poems:*

> *What can we salvage from the ocean's strife*
> *More lovely than these skeletons that lie*
> *Like scattered flowers open to the sky,*
> *Yet not despoiled by their consent to life?*

Anything that can remain true to itself in surrender is a treasure. I keep the broken shell, putting it gently into the plastic cup.

I also collect three drinking straws; a purple hair elastic that I remember as a "scrunchie," the kind of thing my daughters used to hold their ponytails in junior high school; and a bright paper tag from someone's new bathing suit.

I pick up one or two cigarette butts as well, but these are surprisingly hard to spot. With the tobacco gone and the paper disintegrating, what I see are very small oblongs of white, like minuscule bits of birch bark. They look like some kind of natural detritus, and perhaps that is exactly what they are. In any case, they seem to be far along in the journey toward atomization, and hardly worth gathering for disposal. Sometimes it doesn't hurt just to leave things alone.

February 22, 2004 *Evening of the First Day*

I walk again with my cousin who lives near here, on Fort Myers Beach. It was she who made the reservations at the inn, since she knows the owner well. We walk together at the end of the day, both of us wearing wide-brimmed beach hats to shield us from the sunshine, or what is left of it, both of us barefoot on the sand but holding our shoes in one hand while leaving the other free to pick up and examine shells as we walk and talk.

Fifty years ago our mothers did the same thing in the same

place. They were sisters, my mother the older, her mother the younger, just as I and my cousin are.

We walk up the beach in silence, but in harmony, as the sandpipers ahead of us move like a corps of ballet dancers, keeping time to some rhythm inaudible to us.

February 23, 2004 *Morning of the Second Day*

Today's morning walk is earlier, and there are no Jet Skis or life preservers to be seen on the beach, and fewer people on the sands. Those who are here tend to be just walking along, as I am, although one or two are running, or are walking in some deliberate way. Their arms and legs, clearly, have been designated instruments for morning exercise.

A few hardy parents are already digging in the sand with their young children, and one obvious grandmother is cooing enthusiasm as she points out shells to a very young child who is holding her hand happily and paying no attention to her words.

I don't see yesterday's heron, or his fisherman either. I walk in the opposite direction from where they stood, thinking this will give me a new perspective. I have barely begun to walk, with my old, worn Birkenstocks in one hand and my new orange straw beach bag over my shoulder, when I see heron tracks. They are right in front of my feet, on the wet sand: heron tracks within the imprint of a large man's shoe—I'd say size eleven, or even size twelve.

I immediately imagine that the heron has followed the fisherman home for dinner. Or maybe breakfast? Both sets of tracks look recent. Soon they vanish, not into the fisherman's kitchen but into a stretch of dry and traceless white sand.

I now have several shells clicking against one another in the palm of my right hand, along with the broken one in the plastic cup. I am amused that one of these is the moon shell of my mother's third chapter in *Gift from the Sea*. Yesterday I was so sure that these would have disappeared from Captiva's beaches by now.

Yet here it is, a perfect specimen: "On its smooth symmetrical face is pencilled with precision a perfect spiral, winding inward to the pinpoint center of the shell, the tiny dark core of the apex, the pupil of the eye. It stares at me, this mysterious single eye—and I stare back."

I am not staring at the moon shell, but I am smiling at it. So you are still here after all, friend of my mother. How very glad I am to see you.

I have found three unbroken channeled whelks this morning, and enough bright, white, ribbed "angel wings," as we used to call them, to take several very small souls to heaven, maybe the souls of house mice. My mother loved house mice.

I finally turn to walk back along the beach toward the path I took this morning from my own little cottage, and just before I reach the place where I leave the sand for the pine needles, I look toward the surf and see the heron. There is no fisherman, just the heron alone, standing in the shallow water. Something in his stillness makes me edgy today. I don't know why.

Do something, I ask him silently. Catch a fish. Make a move, you beauty. Don't just stand there. But he stands there. And stands there, and stands there. I wait, he stands, I wait some more. Finally I give up.

Then, just as I take my first steps onto the pine-needle path toward home, the heron stretches out with his whole head and neck, out and over and around and under his wing, and scratches vigorously at something invisible there. A flea?

Okay. Fine. See you later.

February 23, 2004 *Evening of the Second Day*

I take my afternoon walk later today, when the beach is quieter and the colors of sky and sea and sand are blending together: lavender to pale blue to soft aqua to brown to ivory, where I am walking.

There is a light breeze, and the walkers have longer sleeves than they usually do. A young woman in a red dress, wearing a little cone-shaped red straw hat that looks Japanese to me, carries a baby, wearing a white hat, down toward the shore. I greet them, admire the hats, and continue on.

I see the heron again, this time standing on the beach halfway between shore and tree line. He stands between me and a woman about my age who is sitting in a beach chair. She and I smile at one another across the bird, but we don't speak. Stillness calls for silence. I walk on.

Suddenly, though, the heron is in the air. What seems odd is that he is not flying up and away, but low across the beach, just ahead of me as I walk, slowly winging down the stretch of sand directly in my path and parallel to the shore.

About ten yards ahead of me, he flaps and lands, stops and stands, immobile again. I watch him carefully but I don't stop walking. Not this time. I walk right past him, see if I care. All the same, I glance sideways, surreptitiously, studying every glossy feather as I pass. He pretends, of course, that we've never met.

In a little while I turn around and walk toward home, thinking of dinner. Soon I pass a group of people, including the woman with the red hat and her baby, gathering around the heron in the place where he stands, just as I left him.

Offended by so much attention, perhaps, he moves away. He moves slowly, I see now, with a noticeable limp.

"He is losing a foot," an old man explains, turning to me as I pause at the edge of the circle of people. Losing? It's an odd choice of words. Is the bird's foot about to drop off? Or did I detect a German accent?

The crowd presses closer in its concern, but by now the heron has had enough. It raises itself up and flies off, low and slow, down the beach again. It passes right over my head, and I can see as it flies over me that one leg is indeed missing a foot, but it is evident that the foot has been missing for some time. Even from below, in a brief glimpse, I can tell that there is no wound on the lower part of the leg. There is just a neat and final ending, in nothing, at the bottom of the heron's long dark limb.

"I think he's okay," I observe, speaking with no authority except that of instinct. "I've seen him before, and I think he's fine." And it's true, I do.

With relief, the group relaxes and begins to disperse. Then a young girl asks me something about the seaweed she has seen on the beach. Oh, dear! I have become the resident expert in her eyes, when I am neither resident nor expert in any way. I admit my ignorance, smile a farewell, and walk home.

February 24, 2004 *Morning of the Third Day*

Today as I leave the pine-needle path on my approach to the beach, I spot the heron immediately, just in front of me and in the waves near shore. But he moves rapidly, I see, picking up one perfectly intact foot after the other: left foot, right foot, up and then down in a fastidious two-step, always keeping the same distance between himself and the people on the sand. This is not the same bird.

I give him plenty of space, and start to walk in another direction, irritating a couple of gulls in my path. They fluff and puff and fatten themselves into the importance of feathered admirals, strutting the decks of seagull protocol. To me they look simultaneously impressive and absurd. So many things are contradictory, so many truths double-sided, in this world.

I pick up a shell, another exquisitely worn, imperfect whelk, broken long ago and shaped by time and tides, again, into a form that speaks to me first of mortality and its associated sadness, then of things eternally true. How comforting these things are, whether mathematical or emotional: Fibonacci's spiral, recurrent in nature in so many things I love: a seashell, a pine tree, my mother's words and her silence, coexisting.

I knew my mother's presence as a constant in my life for more than fifty years. Now I know her absence in the same way, and I will know it for as long as I live. But more important than either knowledge is her place in my heart, which does not change.

She is gone forever. She will be with me forever. Everything changes, everything stays the same. Is it cynicism to believe this, or is it reverence?

I have a favorite photograph of my mother, one that I keep with me all the time. In this picture she is in her late eighties, still looking bright-eyed and very pretty, smiling directly at the camera.

I bet she can't see much, though. She has done exactly what I do when someone takes a photograph of me. She has removed her glasses. She is holding the lavender stems of the glasses in her two hands, and her hands are resting lightly in the lap of a cotton dress I remember very well. It, too, is lavender, with a print of small white flowers. She is wearing a pink sweater, too, over the dress.

I know exactly where and when this picture was taken: in Florida, on Fort Myers Beach, where my cousin lives now. It was twenty years after my father's death, and more than forty years following the publication of *Gift from the Sea*. She had already suffered several small strokes, and I know that her mind wandered in confusion at least some of the time. Yet she faces the camera with characteristic openness, a nicely human touch of feminine vanity that I share, and as I know very well from having shared much of this time with her, she looks out at the world with a kind of eager delight.

I keep this photograph with me because it reminds me of the many ways in which my mother lights my way through the world, even now. I have taped to the back of the photo a fragment of a poem by Galway Kinnell, "The Last Hiding Places of Snow," that expresses what I feel about her:

> *I have always felt*
> *anointed by her love, its light*
> *like sunlight*
> *falling through broken panes*
> *onto the floor*
> *of a deserted house: we may go, it remains,*
> *telling of goodness of being, of permanence.*
>
> *So lighted I have believed*
> *I could wander anywhere,*
> *among any foulnesses, any contagions,*
> *I could climb through the entire empty world*
> *and find my way back, and learn again to be happy.*

At the end of my walk I find my way back again along this beach in Captiva. I pass this morning's perfect heron, and I remember the heron I saw yesterday evening, flying before me on powerful wings, one foot missing.

I hold my newest and most beautiful broken shell in one hand, and it rests there, light as a heron's feather in my palm. I walk slowly, thinking about things broken and things whole, and wondering if there is really all that much difference between the two.

8. *Minding the Clutter, Cluttering the Mind*

Sooner or later I should probably face up to the task of weeding and sorting the accumulations of my cluttered lifetime. I've been involved with a couple of estates recently, so I know that it would be a gift to my children to spare them more work than necessary when I'm gone, and when I say "gone," I mean "dead and gone." Regardless of my final destination, I don't want to be embarrassed there because I have left behind a mess for my bewildered heirs to clean up.

I am fully aware that there are some things I have been unable to part with over the years that will have less allure for my children than they have for me. I am referring not only to furniture, books, papers, paintings, and knickknacks dating back as far as my children's childhood or even my own, but also lesser artifacts, in worse shape: ancient, mangy stuffed animals; outgrown but unre-cyclable baby sleep-suits; mud-colored kindergarten paintings with dried paint flaking into dust on paper stiff with age.

How much of this do I want my kids to have to go through, years hence? How much of it do I want to deal with myself, a little further down the road? My ambition for the future is to be a cheerful old woman with a certain amount of charm and style, enjoying life as it unfolds for as long as it does. I haven't yet decided whether the style will be Gracious Old Lady or what one of my brothers refers to as "Elderbabe." Both roles are tempting, both will require some advance planning and some new clothes, but as I step into my next stage of life, I don't want to be constantly tripping over the detritus of the last one.

Or do I?

The trouble with me is that I've never known what to let go of and what to keep. I don't know what is important, or maybe it is that I don't always know the difference between what is important to me personally and what is important to my life objectively. I've learned, because of having to replace some of them, that I need to hang on to certain documents, which I will be asked to produce from time to time: birth certificates, marriage and driver's licenses, deeds, titles, legal and medical and dental records, things like that.

I have also learned to know the ambiguity inherent in the keeping and caring for animals and children. However much I may care for them, any "keeping" of these living creatures is temporary. We live in the ebb and flow of connection and disconnection, moving between tight embrace and full surrender, whether we like it or not. Children nurse at the breast and cling to our hands, and then grow up and leave us. That's their job.

As for the animals, I have welcomed exuberant puppies into our home with enthusiasm and watched them die as old dogs not so many years later, in the adventure of dignity and trust that includes a beloved pet and the owner who will outlive it. The birth of new spring lambs here every year is wet chaos followed by delight, as we watch these young animals romping in the fields in May. A year further on, or less, those frolicking spring lambs are adult sheep, and we eat them.

One way or another, the children and animals come and go, like everything else in life that we think is ours.

But isn't there something I can keep, at least for the present? Among all the clutter, and beyond the official documents, what do I have that is so meaningful to me that I will exempt it from late-life spring cleaning? If I had to leave my home today and never return, what would I take with me?

I know one or two people who have lost a home to fire. Years later, these people said that what they missed most were the personal things: photographs, letters, journals, family records. Regardless of financial circumstances, it is not the conventionally valuable items that we mourn at such times, not furniture, jewelry, artwork, but instead those small, unique objects that remind us who we are and where we came from and by whom we have been loved. I know I could give up the TV set and the paintings, even the books (that would be harder), but to see my children's early photographs go up in flames, or my letters from my mother and my sister, would break my heart.

Each person grows accustomed to living with his or her own particular treasure. When our family went through my mother's belongings after her death, it became clear to me that she had treated the stones and feathers and shells of her life with just as much reverence as the china, crystal, and silver she had inherited or acquired over the years—in fact, with a good deal more reverence, because she kept the things she really loved with her in her home, and stored everything else.

In a storage facility in Stamford, Connecticut, in September of 2001, we found box after box of gifts from my parents' wedding in 1929 carefully packed away. It looked to me as if most of these gifts had been resting undisturbed in their original nest of tissue paper for almost seventy-five years, with even the gift cards intact. There were crystal bowls and silver candlesticks, plump hand-painted pottery tureens, fragile teacups and saucers, and a large collection that was listed in the estate inventory as "Assembled Set of Georgian Feather Edge Pattern Flatware—most from the late 18th Century by various makers." That was the silver.

We opened and explored box after box, a doubly strange process because we arrived at the storage unit to examine our inheritance early on the morning of September 11, during a week we had reserved with the proprietors long beforehand. Terrible news was breaking over the airwaves as we entered the facility, with broadcasts over the car radio as we drove, and up-to-the-minute news relayed by the elevator operator as we ascended to the area where our mother's possessions were stored, and TV bulletins at the nearby diner where we went for lunch. We had only those few days when my brothers and I were together and the appraiser could come to look at the material, so we kept on working.

It was good to be working, because a sense of unreality pervaded that day and the days that followed. Work made sense: hands working with objects and with lists and with other hands, writing things down, unpacking and packing, lifting and moving. The objects themselves, beautiful as some of them were as they emerged from the wrappings of the past, had little meaning for me in the context of buildings falling and people dying in New York City, maybe thirty miles away from the place where I stood counting teaspoons.

Later, when I could think about things again, I was amazed at the sheer quantity of possessions that had lain unused for so long. I knew that my parents had stored some of my mother's inheritance from her own mother, who died in the 1950s, but I had never thought much about this stored material. In fact, about a dozen years before our mother died, when she had become too frail to manage her own affairs, my sister and I joked about the mysterious monthly bills we had to pay for "Storage." Our mother could not recall what these were for, so Anne and I made up a riddle:

Q: What is it that is not valuable enough to keep, too valuable to give, sell, or throw away, but just valuable enough to be worth paying monthly storage fees for fifty years?

A: I can't remember.

Our mother's death in 2001 came eight years after Anne's, and by the time I was counting teaspoons in Stamford, I understood the situation differently. Our mother had paid to store this collection of valuables for all those years because it was family treasure, and she was its guardian. While her daughters laughed, she was saving treasure for us.

The silver and the china and the crystal did not conform to her own notion of treasure, I knew. She had grown up with all of this, but when I knew her she treasured other things: the huge, pink-mouthed horse conch shell from Captiva, which sat with the gleaming authority of any crystal vase or silver bowl on top of the Korean chest in the front hallway of her home in Connecticut; the rippled blue glass vase on the windowsill, just behind the big two-sided desk that once belonged to her father and now belongs to her son Land, holding a single branch of forsythia she had clipped with her ever-present garden clippers during her daily walk with the dog; the "lucky stone," on her bedside table, a hand-sized, sea-worn rock from the beaches of North Haven, Maine, with a ring of white quartz running around its middle, unbroken. Shells and stones and feathers, the shapes of bare branches or driftwood from the beach, all of these she loved.

I, too, love shells and stones and driftwood, but rarely feathers. I have kept hens for so many years that I take feathers for granted like the cobwebs and dust in the old windows high above the barn loft. I remove feathers from fresh-laid eggs in the henhouse when I go out to check the nesting boxes in the morning. When Nat shovels the floor of the sheep stalls after winter, there are feathers mixed in with the manure. The feathers on our farm are neither interesting nor clean, so I don't save them.

On the other hand, I don't object to having a few of those featheredged teaspoons my mother left us, and I love the brace of ornate silver candlesticks that came from her 1929 wedding gift collection, and the dishes that were part of a set I remember seeing at Sunday dinners at my grandmother's home in Englewood, New Jersey, when I was a child.

Still, I am my mother's daughter, and I have carefully put away in a closet most of my share of the treasure my mother saved for her children in storage. The teapots and the goblets and the plates will go to my children during my lifetime: at a wedding, to welcome a new baby, to celebrate a young couple's first home. I have at last learned from my mother that family treasure is to be respected, guarded carefully, and always passed on.

What is not treasure, however, is clutter, and I have an awful lot of it. I'm sure I'm not the only person my age who is thinking about household accumulations that we should go through and dispose of in a reasonable manner. While I was thinking about this process, it occurred to me that there was another kind of clutter I have lived with for just as many years. I can simplify my life by getting rid of some of the clutter in my house, but what am I going to do about all the clutter I've collected in my mind?

Only a small portion of my life is lived on the outside, after all, with the candlesticks and the seashells. The rest is internal. What have I packed away in the inmost nooks and crannies of my brain, let alone buried deep in the murky realms of my emotions? Isn't it equally important to jettison some of that old stuff? This might not affect my heirs, but wouldn't it perk up my Gracious Old Lady/Elderbabe years? Of course it would, but what a job it would be! The attic of the mind is bad enough, with the dust and junk of remembered events and experiences. Far worse is the entrenched grit and slime of the basement, the place Yeats calls "the foul rag and bone shop of the heart." If I really wanted to simplify my life in any meaningful way, I'd have to go through this stuff, too. Where would I start? I think with the mind.

Some people may really have "orderly minds." I've heard of such people, so I try to believe they exist, but I'm inclined to believe that these people show the world and themselves only a little of their mental activity. The rest, too disturbing to be acceptable to the nervous housewife of consciousness, moves in its own erratic patterns underground. I suspect that my father was this kind of person, even with his many accomplishments and despite the elaborately ordered arrangements he made in his own life and in the lives of other people. I wonder whether he feared chaos, and whether the chaos he feared was within. What a burden it must have been, if this were true: my father's lifetime effort to keep disorder at bay. He must have felt disorder threatening the borders of his being all the time like a hungry wolf whining at the door.

I have wondered, too, how a person like my father could have created a child like me. My mind is not orderly at all. I am usually able to get things done when they need doing, but my mind is rampant with disorder at every level, crammed with bits of information and associations that go back through the decades: words and faces, actual memories and memories of dreams, fragments of stories both true and imagined, valued individual verses or entire poems and songs memorized from the *Fireside Book of Folk Songs,* which once sat on my mother's piano and now sits on mine, jingles from radio and television ads of the 1950s and 1960s—*Brush-a Brush-a Brush-a, Get the new Ipana*—and so on.

Beyond this mental messiness, I was born puny and anemic, a terrible physical specimen. My father, who was a universal donor, gave me a pint of blood at my birth. Now and then he would say to me half jokingly, "Remember that pint of blood!" Once, exasperated, I offered to give it back to him, but he just chuckled.

I was lucky. As the youngest child in our large family I was in the fortunate position that many younger children enjoy with older parents. I had no conflicts with my mother—I don't know anybody who did—and very few with my father, though like all of his children I had to endure his tediously long, often repetitive lectures, which took place in his office, downstairs in the old house in Connecticut. The office was a kind of closed-in porch with stone walls and a big arched window looking out on Long Island Sound. I would look toward the water and the small islands of the cove, letting my father's voice rumble and roll over my head. Or, looking right into his eyes as if I were really listening to him, I would identify the words and phrases that my sister, Anne, used when making fun of him behind his back—"downfall of civilization" and "punk design."

He tried to teach us many things, as fathers do. But when he taught me things by lecturing, it was not at all like being taught to drive a car or to shoot a rifle, and I was often pretending to pay attention until—finally!—it was over.

I seem to remember a painting on the wall of my father's office, of an apple orchard in the sunshine. I sometimes looked at the painting instead of the view when he was lecturing me. There was a sense of golden light in the painting; the tiny leaves and bright red apples appeared to glow, and the grass was very green. I think I remember him telling me that he had painted this picture himself, but I'm not absolutely sure. It may be one of those memories that comes from a dream. If not, and if my father really painted that picture, then there was something else about him that he kept hidden inside. I think if he had let it out more often, that wolf would have been eating out of his hand.

But, as I say, it may have been a dream.

The flotsam in my own mind exists there democratically. It is neither ranked nor "prioritized," a word that I hear frequently and often find absurd, because it assumes that first things can always be made to go first, and second things second, and last things last, as in the French nursery song about three hens in single file, which my sister sang to her children in an old house in the Dordogne region of France, to the tune of "Twinkle, Twinkle, Little Star":

> *Quand trois poules vont aux champs*
> *La première va devant*
> *Le second suit la première*
> *La troisième va derrière*
> *Quand trois poules vont aux champs*
> *La première va devant.*
>
> *When three hens go out to play*
> *The first hen will lead the way*
> *Then the second goes behind her.*
> *The third one? At the end we'll find her.*
> *When three hens go out to play*
> *The first hen will lead the way.*

It's a charming little song, with a touch of Gallic tongue-in-cheek as those three plump hens set out together in a neat line. (Rhode Island Reds, I like to think.) But I have kept chickens for a great many years, as I said, and I have yet to see three hens lined up anywhere unless they are asleep on a roost or packaged in the poultry section of the supermarket. Hens don't walk in line.

My mind, like our barnyard, is chock-full of chickens. My thoughts scatter in all directions if I try to force a one-two-three order upon my unruly flock. I do try to perceive, at least, which birds are in the barnyard on any given day: small brown hens gently clucking over new-hatched baby chicks? A strutting, crowing rooster with delusions of grandeur? I can't control them, but I like to know what's in there.

A friend once told me a story she heard about Buddhist meditation practice. The tale compared the constant activity of our thinking mind to the movements of a monkey in the jungle. The monkey is in a clearing, a verdant, quiet space surrounded by trees and open to the sky. But the monkey is so agitated and so active that he cannot stay where he is or even see this beautiful place. He keeps racing around the clearing and running up and down the surrounding trees. Meditation practice, my friend was told, is just a matter of finding the monkey wherever he is, and bringing him back again, and again, and again, each time just setting him gently on the ground.

I like this story because it gives such a vivid picture of the hungrily active nature of thought. But for me, a native New Englander, monkeys are a little too exotic. I'll stick with my brain-chickens, those restless Rhode Island Reds.

My chickens don't climb trees any more than they line up. But they can sing! Without being invited to do so, whenever they feel like it, they'll sing me French nursery rhymes or Anglo-Saxon sea chanties ("Haul Away, Joe," "Sloop John B") or themes from Walt Disney movies: "Whistle While You work" from *Snow White* is a favorite, and I always hear it in the form of a 1952 political tune based on the Disney classic. I'd dearly love to delete this from my eclectic consciousness, but I cannot. It goes like this:

> *Whistle while you work*
> *Stevenson's a jerk*
> *Eisenhower has the power*
> *Whistle while you work.*

I can't forget it, even though both my parents voted for Adlai Stevenson, not because they disliked General Eisenhower, who won the election, but because they had read Stevenson's speeches and writings. They thought he was an extraordinary man, the kind of person who *should* be president of the United States but rarely gets elected. My father told me that he voted for a Democrat for president that year because of Stevenson, even though he "tended" to vote Republican. He did not think of himself as a Republican or a Democrat, just a voter with certain tendencies. The aberration of 1952 was my mother's fault. She had left a book of Stevenson's writings by my father's bedside, and he had read it.

I had to look up the year of that election, but the song remains in my memory intact, more than fifty years later. I'd like to wring *that* brain-chicken's neck!

Some hens in my flock are more pious than others. They sing hymns, and I'm very glad they do. Whatever one might believe, or not, hymns are good for the body as well as the soul, filling the lungs and swelling the chest at sad times like funerals, when it feels as if everybody needs more oxygen. Some of my hens recite psalms, too: "For the Beauty of the Earth" and "A Mighty Fortress Is Our God" bump up against "The Lord Is My Shepherd," the Prayer of St. Francis, "Lord, Make Me an Instrument of Thy Peace," and the Quaker tune "Simple Gifts." Present forever is the 121st Psalm, "I will lift up mine eyes unto the hills, from whence cometh my help . . ." My mother's family called this "The Morrow Prayer." For me, as for them, I think, this psalm evokes the sea-and-landscape of the Maine islands in Penobscot Bay, and the Camden Hills beyond.

And then there is the poetry, from Robert Frost to Robert Service: "Some say the world will end in fire" and "A bunch of the boys were whooping it up in the Malemute saloon." Without knowing the author or the provenance, I could sing all the verses to the saga of the fateful meeting between those two great warriors, Abdul Abulbul Amir and Ivan Skavinsky Skavar. Just ask me.

I dredge some of this up from the pool of memory from time to time to entertain myself or my friends—I'm not the only one who remembers *Brush-a Brush-a Brush-a*. The other collection I have, as useless as bottle caps in a box, is numbers: passwords and combination padlocks and locker keys, street addresses that were obsolete half a century ago, and telephone numbers, like the one for my great-uncle in Fort Myers Beach, Florida. We called him on Sunday nights. One of the children would begin the process, and when it was my turn to place the call, my father would instruct me to speak slowly and "enunciate." I'd stand very still, as if posture mattered, in the little kiosklike area downstairs where the telephone was located. I'd say into the receiver, "I'd . . . like . . . to make . . . a . . . long . . . distance . . . call, please, to Fort Myers Beach, Florida. The number is MOhawk 3-2502." The operator would connect me and then my great-uncle's thin, high cowboy voice would come on the line—I always thought of this man, Charles Land, as a very old cowboy— and we would talk briefly, then I'd hand the phone to the next brother or sister.

Along with my great-uncle's phone number I have all our unlisted Lindbergh family telephone numbers in Darien, Connecticut, where I grew up. One number succeeded the other over the years, and all of them were secret, sacred, unforgettable. When you are taught to memorize your home phone number and never to reveal it except to close relatives and maybe the family doctor, you don't forget that number.

First it was a simple string of digits, 52350. Then it was OLiver 5-9510, until OLiver turned back into numbers again with 655, and our part of Connecticut adopted the area code 203. My mother's phone number in Connecticut at the end of her life was 203-655-2229. These numbers are all meaningless now, but they

still perch on the roost of memory with weighty importance. Seeing them on this page sends a ripple of guilt through me to this
day. My parents are long dead, the houses we lived in have been
sold or torn down, but I have revealed our secret numbers to the
world, and still my Lindbergh training whispers to me, *Oh, boy, are
you going to get in trouble!*

Some of my chickens, I have to confess, have flown the coop,
especially the more recent additions. It shocks me to realize that I
know my great-uncle's telephone number in Florida in 1958 and
the name of every child in the second-grade class I taught in 1970,
but I can't come up with the first name of my new neighbor's
husband, whom I met last week. I know that this is a common
phenomenon for those of us who are getting older (and we all
know who we are) but it is unsettling anyway.

Maybe the trouble with my brain is that it's just too crowded in
there. Is there some way to set some of this cerebral poultry free?
I'm thinking now about those numbers I don't need anymore, the
ones that keep popping up in my head and volunteering useless
information, like overeager students who want to show you how
much they know about everything, regardless of relevance.

Some numbers can be recycled, like my old five-digit Harvard
Coop number, critical for purchases at the big bookstore in Harvard Square when I was living in Cambridge in the late 1960s, but
not at all useful in my life in northern Vermont nowadays. Still,
I've never forgotten it, so I use it as a personal identification code
when I need one.

Some numbers have finally deleted themselves, after fifty years
of disuse. I realized the other day that I can no longer remember
the telephone number of my best friend in elementary school, the
one who moved away at the end of fifth grade. I don't remember
her dog's name, either, or her grandmother's, or the name of her
big sister's boyfriend. He played the saxophone and had a large

Adam's apple and was very handsome. I'll remember his name if I work on it.

Beyond the remembered numbers and songs, behind the forgotten names and addresses, below the level of conscious accumulation, there are some ancient feelings lurking, but as I get older I see these creatures in my mind with the tolerance of long familiarity. This dispels at least some of their distracting force. I know by now that it doesn't serve me well to squander my energy on self-righteousness or malice or fear or irritation, or even guilt—one of my oldest and most demanding friends. I notice, too, that a number of older people I know, though by no means all of them, have taken this same path. It is clear that for these people fears and anxieties have lessened with age, jealousies and resentments have disappeared or at least have lost their sharp edges, worn smooth with time and experience. I admire these people. I would love to follow their example.

My husband disagrees with me. He says he loves his complaints, and hopes he can keep them all and gather some more. He wants to roar and rant and rave through his golden years. He is a big man with bushy eyebrows, well built for a curmudgeonly role, and I hope he enjoys it. I know that however curmudgeonly he may get, he will not join the company of those who spend their last years clinging grimly to their grudges: a sister stole a boyfriend sixty-five years ago, a business achievement went unrecognized, a book was never reviewed.

It is all too easy to cherish ideas as if they were companions, and to think about what *should* have happened but didn't, and how life *should* be but isn't. Too many of us lose the minute-by-minute glory of our own lives as we concentrate upon struggles that were over long ago, or chase elusive dreams set in the future.

On the other hand, it isn't so easy to feel glorious every minute, and I bet it doesn't get any easier as one gets older. I remember complaining about what I saw as my elderly mother's grumpy unwillingness to *enjoy* life when she was very old and frail. She had always been such a lover of life; now she rarely smiled, hardly ever showed enthusiasm or eagerness about anything.

"When is she ever *happy?*" I asked my friend Ann Cason, my mother's wise and thoughtful caregiver.

"Oh, I'd say between five and six o'clock in the evening," Ann replied with a smile. She stopped my tirade in its tracks because this observation was so true. It had always been true. Five to six in the evening was the tea hour at my mother's house. At that time, for as long as I'd known her, my mother had set aside everything she was doing to go into the kitchen and bring out a tray covered with a brightly patterned cloth and holding a steaming teapot and some white translucent cups and saucers ("bone china," I believe) and a few of those featheredged silver teaspoons.

Along with our tea, and sugar and lemon and maybe a little milk, we would have a small plate of what she called "a little something sweet at the end of the day": cinnamon toast wedges, lemon-flavored muffins, in Switzerland a basket of brioche or a large, round cuchaule, a loaf of light, sweet bread. We would sit with our cups of tea, enhanced with sugar or cream or lemon or a combination of these, and I would reach out with as much polite restraint as I could muster for that "little something sweet." We would sip and munch and talk until it was time to put the tea things away and take a walk with the dog, and then think about dinner.

Sometimes, if the talk was good enough, the tea hour would blend gently into the sherry hour, with cheese and crackers and Pedro Domecq in cold three-inch pewter tumblers, or in globe-shaped stemless glasses of the same size, which I held in my hand and tipped slowly from side to side so that whenever I looked down I could see the lines of my palm through liquid amber.

My mother was happy between five and six in the evening.

What more did I expect from her, and why did I expect it? I, too, am happy at certain moments each day. Between six o'clock and seven o'clock in the morning, if my hands are curled around a cup of hot coffee with plenty of milk and sugar in it, and if I am sitting by the window where I can watch a chickadee perching on a branch of the lilac bush my friend Gretchen gave me after Ben was born, and if Nat is watching the BBC news and grumbling about the government, then I am perfectly happy, any day of the year.

I am happy sitting in my chair here, now, writing and breathing with the house quiet and the dog asleep on the floor. I am happy with the slight crick in my neck and the forward tilt of my body, the familiarity of my left hand, my writing hand, moving the pen across the yellow-lined paper, the glance of my eye as it follows the pen and catches a glimpse of the uneven boards of the wooden floor at my feet. All of this makes me happy. I have none of the exalted ambitions I had when I was younger. Where did they go?

As a child I loved princesses, and would leave on my mother's desk almost daily my penciled drawings of ladies in ball gowns, who wore very tall and beribboned cone-shaped hats. Fifty-some years later, I would rather be the un-princess, working backward through the fairy stories and reversing the usual plots to find my own happy endings. I'd rather be the goose girl on one of those old European farms in paintings than any of the gowned and gorgeous ladies, would rather stay home with the mice and the pumpkins than wear glass slippers at the palace ball, and if I had the gift of spinning—it isn't as easy as it looks—I would not want to spin straw into gold. That sounds like a very dangerous talent. You could end up spending your life in Fort Knox. I say let straw be straw.

There is something to be said for cleaning up a lifetime of clutter, whether in the house or in the mind. As I think more about the project, though, I'm more and more doubtful that I'll ever really get it done. My intentions are honorable, but I know me. The more old stuff I get rid of in my house, my head, or my heart, the more new stuff I'll accumulate: books and letters, candlesticks, stones and shells, chickens, grandchildren. I will clean out a closet or two, and I may let go of some outdated ideas and feelings, but others will come along to fill the vacancies.

And when the time comes to go through my possessions after I've died, I hope my children will do what I did after my own mother's death. They will keep what they want to keep of the treasure that was left to them, however they choose to define it, and they will put some things aside for their own children. Then they will, I hope, throw away my stones, shells, feathers, kindergarten paintings, stuffed animals, and all the rest of it. They'd better get rid of my clutter. By then they'll need the space for their own.

9. Brain Tumor Diary

At first it seemed almost ridiculous. Just ten days after I finished writing the chapter about the excess accumulations in my mind, I found out I had a brain tumor. "Take a deep breath," our doctor and old friend Tim Thompson advised. "This probably isn't *super*-bad." The tumor was most likely a meningioma, almost certainly benign and very slow-growing. It could have been in my brain for a long time, twenty years or more. I learned later through a friend's research on the Internet that this kind of tumor tends to be found in women over fifty, and I was told by several people over the course of the next six months that the prognosis was excellent, barring the unforeseen.

Each time someone uses this word "unforeseen," I remember how my father at the end of his lectures to his children often gave us a kind of universal warning in the accents of the Minnesota childhood he never entirely left behind him. "Don't forget the unforeseen," he would caution. He pronounced it "un-fuss-*eeen* . . . ," a drawn-out hum of a word that came from deep in his chest and left the sound of itself suspended in the air after he spoke, like the twang of the lowest strings of a guitar.

My thoughts and feelings about the brain tumor over the months were woven with all the other things recorded in my diary of the time, not because I wasn't scared and apprehensive—I was both, and I had a delayed, mercifully brief bout of depression a few months after the intensity of the crisis had passed—but I found it impossible to isolate the seriousness of the medical situation, however serious it might be, from what my mother used to call "the ongoingness of life." I suppose this might be labeled Denial, in the uppercase vocabulary of Death and Dying literature, but I think these thoughts and feelings were mostly just habit.

To write as honestly as I can in my journals about my everyday life and the thoughts and feelings I have as I go along is an old, tenacious yearning, maybe due to an early discomfort with the oddly intangible enormities of my family history. Or perhaps this effort is just something else my mother left to me: her belief that writing is the way to make life as perceptible as life can be perceived, first by the writer, moment by moment, and then, with luck and patience, by others as well. Through her writing, for as long as she was able to pick up a pen and put her thoughts on paper, my mother confronted all that was most difficult in her life and paid tribute to all that she loved.

For me the effort to write about life is comforting and steadying, though some of the outpourings may be tedious for any reader but myself. Did I really need to fill thirty pages with observations on the birth and feeding of lambs this spring, after thirty years of sheep keeping? I guess I did.

The brain tumor diagnosis did not change my journal-writing habits. For one thing, aside from the initial episode of lost consciousness that sent me to the doctors for tests and consultations, I felt well, not ill, throughout the whole experience. I had expected that the problem would be related to my seizure medication and an old scar on the brain from a head injury in my twenties, so I was surprised to know there was something else in there, too. But it seemed clear early on that we would have time to consider various treatments, which would not have been true had the tumor been fast-growing or malignant.

A good friend of mine named Judy Kendall plays tennis with our doubles group once a week. She was diagnosed with a larger brain tumor just before I was. The doctors at first thought that Judy's tumor might be benign, like mine. But it was not. By the time I learned about my own tumor, Judy had been through brain surgery and was undergoing radiation and chemotherapy. She continued to play tennis with our doubles group most Fridays starting only a month or so after surgery, and we often play as partners. If we lose a set we refer to ourselves as the "Brain Drain."

It was Judy, a financial consultant and one of the funniest people I know, who gave me the most information about hospitals and treatments and about the disconcerting tasks neurological patients are asked to perform: *Can you count backward from one hundred by sevens / name fifteen animals / touch your nose and then my fingers / walk a straight line?* (At a certain point you wonder if the next test will be a Breathalyzer.) Judy gave me courage by making me laugh, and in return I composed a brain tumor poem in her honor. For this tribute I appropriated the rhyme scheme of my next-to-be-published children's book, which happened to be a little story in verse about a boy and his grandmother. The grandmother has Alzheimer's disease or some other kind of brain degeneration resulting in memory loss. I wrote the verse soon after the death of my mother in 2001, but like all my children's books this was designed as a "picture book" for very young children, so it took some time for the publisher, Candlewick Press, to find the right artist, for the artist to do her work, and then for the book to make its way through the publication process.

My Little Grandmother Often Forgets was published in April 2007, three months after I'd been through my own surgery. I may be oversensitive, but what with completing the chapter about my cluttered mind just before the brain tumor diagnosis, and seeing the demented grandmother book appear in print just after brain surgery, I felt as if my whole life was a brain sandwich that year. Writing the poem for Judy helped a lot.

My Little Brain Tumor *(For Judy, my inspiration!)*

My little brain tumor lives in my head
They say it's not nasty, or else I'd be dead.

It's in my meninges. It looks like a dot
Or a snail with a tail, or a small Rorschach blot.

My little brain tumor showed on a scan.
I was asked, "Can you see this?" I said, "Yes, I can."

I can see, I can speak, can count backwards from ten.
I can walk a straight line and then walk back again,

I can name fifteen animals, all in a row,
Subtract from one hundred by sevens (that's slow).

I can write, I can work, I can wander about,
I can drive, but I don't, just in case I pass out.

My little brain tumor doesn't look scary.
It's smallish and roundish—the size of a cherry.

It may have to go, though it's shown little malice,
But if I can keep it, I'm calling it Alice.

Judy kept my sense of my own trouble in perspective at a time when it would have been easy to inflate and sensationalize the situation. Medical self-importance is so tempting, and I soon discovered that the effect the two words "brain tumor" have on people is remarkable: "I'm sorry, I can't help you / be there / send a contribution just now. I have a brain tumor." Stunned silence, then instant retreat. With these results it's hard to resist taking advantage of the circumstances. Having a brain tumor, I found out, even a benign one, is like having an excuse note for a permanent absence from school. Better yet, from committee meetings. Best of all, it's a valid excuse, backed up by medical caution. It can be used for a long time, like those "old war wounds" in British novels: the hero grimaces bravely and the heroine knows he's feeling the injury received on the Somme.

Generally, my time with Alice, as I called my tumor (in honor of a small, brave, and charming elderly relative for whom I have great affection), permitted me to live as I always have. I didn't drive and I had many doctor's appointments and hospital visits, but otherwise the routine of my days was virtually intact. For me this makes all the difference.

There have been one or two horrible times in my life, as there are in too many lives, when the "ongoingness" my mother taught me to value was interrupted in a radical way and neither daily rhythms nor the discipline of writing could restore my balance. An event can be so cataclysmic that it pulls its surviving victims right out of life to plummet into a deep and terrible darkness where there is no solid ground and where day-to-day comforts are meaningless. I have learned by living through a few such times, however, that daily life has a strength and a staying power even more persistent than the terrible downward forces of catastrophe. Dailiness outlasts despair. For a while the rhythms of daily life may seem to be submerged, even drowned in disaster, but that is never true. Sooner or later, after mornings and evenings and mornings and evenings and mornings and evenings again, however many of them it takes, and never by dishonoring reality or by displacing grief, never by rushing the inevitability of feeling, meaning always returns.

My brain tumor was not an event of this magnitude. It was a

shock, a worry, a challenge, and probably a greater concern than I would admit until afterward. It became an important element in my life, but as I read my journal of that year I see that there was plenty going on. It is interesting to me to see how different aspects of my life all came into play: apprehension and fear; moments of euphoria (Denial?); local gossip; literary, philosophical, and political commentary, though thankfully not too much of that; and above all reams of writing about my children and animals. I like knowing as I read through the minutiae of farm and family detail how intimately my family was with me at that time, though it is no surprise.

July 15, 2006, Saturday

Sitting on the porch, putting on toenail polish and feeling a slight breeze on a muggy mid-July afternoon. The dogs are stretched out near me, occasionally panting or chewing on sticks (or on what's left of a rocket or mortar from the 4th of July—dogs can eat gunpowder, right?). Nat is circling us grimly on the tractor, Ben came out to visit but has retreated with a slam of the screen door, back into the kitchen.

I spent the morning at the Lyndonville Stars and Stripes Festival, serving as grand marshal in the parade. They asked me through the Cobleigh Library back in the spring. It's the library's 100th anniversary and they thought it would be nice to have an author. I came at 9:00 A.M. to the Kennametal parking lot behind the fire station and got into a gray convertible driven by one of the organizers. A well-organized young woman called Cheryl was the driver, and her 4-year-old son, Dayton, was with us in the car, something I found very reassuring. She gave us both bags of candy to toss out to children along the parade route—through the town and around a couple of blocks back to Powers Park—"Don't throw it all out right away," she warned. "It's a long ride."

I wore a sundress and a wide-brimmed hat, and sat up on the back of the backseat, waving and smiling, especially to small children and to friends, who were laughing at me. Mark Breen, the meteorologist from the Fairbanks

Museum, announced us all as we went by, from Reeve Lindbergh, local author, to a whole bevy of local and state politicians and some area soldiers back from Iraq, who received a presentation in honor of their service. The library had a float (The C. S. Lewis Narnia books were the theme and they won a prize!) as did many area businesses, and there was a wonderful street performance about family farms by the Bread and Puppet Theater, dancing on stilts. The Shriners did figure eights in their little cars and their red fezzes—what is that about?—and finally there were fire engines from all the towns around— Lyndonville, St. Johnsbury, Barnet, Newark, Sheffield, East and West Burke. It was really something. I had a great time.

Wednesday of this week I had an odd thing happen while I was driving Nat's truck, with two friends, Carol Hyman and Caroline DeMaio, in the cab with me. We had three kayaks in back. We were going down Route 5 toward Wells River, and the plan was to cross over the bridge there into New Hampshire, and go kayaking on Long Pond. As I was driving along I felt a little strange. Then I heard Carol and Caroline telling me to pull over, and I did—abruptly—the truck nosed into the bushes on the side of the road (no traffic, thank goodness!). Carol (or Caroline?) went to a nearby house and called Nat, then 911, and an ambulance came—for me!

Apparently I had some sort of lapse or spell or a tiny seizure—I hope not a stroke!—my head turned left, the truck did, too (slowly, Caroline said—I took my foot off the gas pedal, I guess, thank God—into the wrong lane, then it veered back over and I pulled off the road—that part I remember . . . So the ambulance/EMT folks came and checked me out—blood pressure fine, general condition fine ("no findings"). I declined in writing to be hospitalized. Nat came and drove me home in my car. Carol and Caroline followed in the truck, kayaks were unloaded, then we called for a doctor's appointment.

July 28, 2006, Friday

I'm not driving for a while, and in the meantime they want me to do all these tests, EEG and CT scan, a couple of Dilantin levels, others as necessary. So we did a blood test at Corner Medical right away, a CT scan last Friday, a blood test on Wednesday, and an EEG yesterday (Thursday) after staying up all night—they like you to be "sleep-deprived." Carol (Hyman) stayed up all night with me . . . this is a real measure of friendship—I hate staying up all night. We watched Dark Passage, *with Bogart and Bacall (pretty awful, in spite of those two, but fun), and then* Bringing Down the House—*Steve Martin and Queen Latifah—wonderful!*

Tim Thompson called last night and told me my Dilantin level was fine, but he wanted to talk to me about the CT scan—and did. He said this was not "super-bad" so he did not want me to "freak out" (his words), but the CT scan showed "an extremely slow-growing meningioma," not in his opinion malignant . . . not a "———oma: ("cytoblastoma"? something like that) or some other bad "oma"—I think of the lymphoma that killed my father, and the melanoma that killed my sister—there are some bad "omas," I'm well aware. Maybe not mine, but it's hard not to wonder.

It looks completely benign, Tim says, about a centimeter in size (a centimeter around? a centimeter in width? I didn't ask—I was listening). He wants me to go to Dartmouth-Hitchcock and have an MRI, whatever that is—guess I'd better look it up—and an appointment with the neurologist there. Tim said that it was likely the decision would be to do nothing, though one option would be to remove the "oma"—i.e., brain surgery. Hmmmm.

"Take a deep breath," said my good doctor, and I did. I also looked up "meningioma" in the dictionary, and learned that it is described as "a tumor in the meninges, usually found in adults." I think I'll let people know that Tim has ordered a full battery of tests, but that so far he's not terribly worried. I think that's true, and I don't see that it helps anything or anybody, in any way, to start babbling about brain tumors.

7/30/06

The roosters are crowing, and I'm trying to write about their self-importance, comparing it to the absurd fury and tenacity of petty emotions—envy, resentment, irritation—but do the roosters crow for self-importance, or for joy? A day! A day! Another day! God bless the world! God bless me in this lovely place! God Bless! God Bless! God Bless! God bless the world, and me in it. If I do have a little brain tumor, a little oma, God bless it, too—Hello, my oma, let's be friends, we are part of each other, aren't we? In that case, why not exercise affection and embrace ourselves as one thing, not two? I embrace and enfold you, you rest (peacefully, please!) gently in me . . .

"It's good to know what your enemy is," Nat said after a long silence, when I told him Tim's report. But I don't agree . . .

"I don't have enemies," I answered immediately without thinking about it, but it's true. What we grow, inside ourselves, how can any of it be classified as "enemies"? This is all part of what and who we are. There are ways to live with whatever is within us, but I don't think the best way is to declare war, or have enemies. There has to be another way.

8/1/06

I'll tell you something weird. I can think about a brain tumor with equanimity, but panic if I can't find my nail file—I just did.

8/13/06

My brother Scott's birthday yesterday and I called him in Brazil—and he was there! He was glad to hear from me, we talked about all the children, and then he started to talk about pigs—again—The last time I called when I hadn't spoken with him in many months he also talked about pigs. Six months ago it was the razorback peccary and the Shavante Indians, this time it was feral hogs . . . some work he is doing to preserve, control, or ameliorate in some way the condition of feral hogs . . . hogs, not pigs. Happy birthday, dear Scott. I love you.

8/16/06

And brother Jon's birthday today, bless him. Though I wasn't able to talk with him, I think of him on his birthday, always, and of my brother Land in May on his, whether we talk or we don't. I wake up with it, the family

*birthday, it doesn't matter which one—a brother's, my father's, my
mother's—I know immediately, can feel it and my love for that family
member before anything else. It's always been this way. Ansy [Anne] and I
were born the same day so it's harder when the birthday is ours—I wake up
with both of us, want us both here. For a while I didn't want a birthday at
all after she died, not if she couldn't share it anymore. How could I celebrate
only half of us? . . . but Nat's birthday is the following day, so we celebrate
two together still, and Lizzy has put "Ansy-Reeve Day" on the calendar
instead of "Reeve's birthday" for me and for all of us—so it's okay again,
sort of. I'm sad always that one of us is dead, glad always that all of us were
born. Happy birthday, dear Jon. I love you, too!*

9/20/06

*Doctors, tests. Talking and thinking for the last month—(except for a brief trip
to NYC to get Ben started/registered at college)—and it looks as though they
want to take it out. Brain surgery after all. Tim would like us to get a second
opinion, so he has referred us to Dr. Phil Gutin at Memorial Sloan-Kettering
in NYC, an old friend and classmate. We'll see him on October 20th.*

9/23/06

*A little low today, with rain and cloudiness here on the farm, and some
tiredness on my part from the past week: brain tumor talk and arrangements,
an unpleasant letter from the lawyer for one of the men who believes he is my
long-dead brother Charles. (I'm not absolutely sure the man who wrote the
letter is a lawyer. His letterhead looks odd, but he may be a California lawyer
who has more casual, less fancy stationery than I'm familiar with.) The
California Pretender. I'm pretty sure there's only one in California, and one
each in Pennsylvania and Florida, and several in Europe.*

10/5/06

*I've been reading Doris Grumbach's 1993 memoir, Extra Innings, and I
found this on p. 147: "Often at odds, a pride of highly individual women*

and supportive men, sometimes turned away from each other by a word or an act, nonetheless, a family like ours is at its best in adversity. It becomes a single defensive unit against whatever threatens to diminish it, cemented by a kind of disparate love that is as fierce as its occasional animosities." Her family may be fiercer than ours (I'm not betting on it!) but this rings true for us, too.

10/11/06

Kiran Desai, with her novel The Inheritance of Loss, *has won the Booker Prize. Someone just interviewed her on TV, and she's lovely, looks a little like my cousin Connie's daughter Anne Fulenwider. A bashful, laughing, thrilled—but disbelieving—response to this good fortune. Kiran Desai is the youngest female recipient ever, and is clearly both intelligent and unpretentious. The interviewer started asking her whether she thought the prize came because of her work being about the "immigrant experience" in India and then in New York, and on "such a broad canvas," and so forth and so on. She laughed, "Oh, gosh, I don't know!" I wanted to buy her book for that alone—and I did.*

10/16/06

If I'm not careful I'll turn into a brain tumor. That will be all I am, the way one turns into a toothache or a bad case of poison ivy. Everything one experiences is perceived through or in reference to that condition. Over the weekend we had a Lindbergh Foundation/EarthShine Institute meeting at Camp Kieve, in Nobleboro, Maine. [The Charles A. and Anne Morrow Lindbergh Foundation is a Minnesota-based nonprofit organization dedicated to balance between technological progress and the preservation of the environment. The EarthShine Institute is a Florida-based supporting organization for the Lindbergh Foundation, with special emphasis on the legacy of Anne Morrow Lindbergh.] While there, we took a day's field trip by ferry to North Haven, significant to family and aviation history, since my mother's family had a summer home there, and my parents landed their

Lockheed Sirius seaplane in the harbor in 1931, at the beginning of their survey flight charting the great circle route over the North Pole to Asia. Almost the whole time I was a brain tumor, with the occasional lapse when I spontaneously forgot about it to listen to or laugh with somebody.

I was badly afflicted by involuntary blinking—it has been driving me nuts, and two doctors besides Tim have noted this development. I know I often get "twitchy" under stress—facial tics are nothing new—but this blinking involves a burning sensation and a feeling like grit or sand in my eyes: very uncomfortable. Now that I'm home, and perhaps because we've had a couple of real frosts at night (is there an allergic component?) the blinking seems to have calmed down. When I spoke to Tim about it he said it may not have anything to do with the tumor, could be "just a little Tourette's syndrome." ("just," Tim?) I mentioned this to Dr. Vijay M. Thadani, my neurologist, when Nat and I went to see him. He asked quietly if anybody in my family was obsessive-compulsive . . .

"Yes—all of them!" Nat said—which changed the tone of the conversation.

10/19/06

Nat and I are heading to New York by train today, to have my head examined—and about time, too, some might say . . .

10/23/06

It was a good visit . . . the train time was very pleasant with Nat beside me pointing out railcars—"Providence and Worcester . . . now that's interesting!"—and keeping me informed as to the condition of the tracks . . . "It's really bad here—that's why we're going so slowly" . . . Drinking in the scenery: the hills, the fields, and especially the river, his river, the Connecticut, all down its lovely length.

We stayed at the Hotel Pennsylvania, just across from Penn Station (or what's left of it) . . . huge and impersonal, with a lobby as full of people as a bus terminal and thousands of rooms all down the seemingly endless hallways upstairs on the floors where the bedrooms are located. As I walked toward our own room I saw that all the doors to the rooms were made of some bulging, hollow-looking metal ("fire doors," Nat said). Maybe it was my mood, but they all looked like coffins to me.

Fun to be in New York with Nat, though. We walked around a bit, then met Ben under the chandelier in the enormous lobby, our dear son walking toward us through the New York crowds with a big smile on his face . . . We looked for a restaurant that wasn't a sports bar, and almost found one: a steak house with tables and good food and only one big TV on the wall—sports, of course.

Okay, the brain tumor. We saw Tim's friend Dr. Phil Gutin, head of neurosurgery at Memorial Sloan-Kettering Cancer Center, for the second opinion, but first a very nice woman helped us to check in and fill out forms. She told us she had been to Vermont for a fife-and-drum event—she's a drummer and a drum majorette for a fife-and-drum corps, like her father before her (majorette? surely not the father?) and many family members around her. She said that when there's a fife-and-drum parade with twenty-six people in it, usually seventeen of them are members of her family . . .

Then we went up in the elevator to the eighteenth floor and were shown in to the doctor's office, where we waited for two hours. That sounds worse than it was. He had a wonderful view of the East River, with the occasional barge or tugboat (and I think one garbage scow—can that be true, these days? But that's what it looked like, as I remember from Stuart Little*). We assumed that a chief neurosurgeon must have emergencies and delays. The only concern we had came from somebody banging and drilling loudly and crudely—a carpenter or electrician, I hoped, not a doctor—in the room next door.*

Phil Gutin finally came in, with a tousled head of gray hair—boyish, but gray—and a big grin.

"You seem like nice people—why do you hang around with a guy like Tim Thompson?"

He'd seen all the information and the test results, could understand that the situation seemed confusing, but in fact the tumor was small and in a "quiet" part of my brain. (Scott Berg commented later, "There's a quiet part of Reeve's brain?" Thanks a lot, Scott.) And he told us that some people couldn't stand having meningiomas and wanted them out, others preferred to monitor these over time with MRIs, avoiding surgery. "You can't go wrong either way," he said, but did not think radiation made sense in my case. I will call Dartmouth-Hitchcock to make arrangements for surgery as soon as we get home. It just seems right to me, and Nat agrees.

We did not spend a lot of time with Dr. Gutin but somehow he cheered us both up tremendously. We went on to have dinner with Marek [my nephew] and Ben and their gorgeous sweet cousin Wendy Fulenwider, Anne's sister, at a Japanese restaurant called Shabu-Tatsu. Before dinner we went to the Metropolitan Museum, mostly looking at American paintings. I think the St. Johnsbury Athenaeum's Bierstadt is vastly superior to the one I saw at the Met, and I felt very friendly with all the Cropseys and Whittredges and other Hudson River School paintings because of the ones in St. Johnsbury.

I'm feeling pretty calm and content, with a little panic running through me every so often—brain tumor? Even this, it seems, is something I can get used to. Oh, why not—

11/5/06

Frost for the last few mornings, and Nat has pumpkins and leeks and endives all over the kitchen floor, to save them from the killing cold. He has had some wonderful farm dreams: there was a whole flock of tame wild turkeys, easy to cuddle with and hold in his arms; his brussels sprouts grew eight feet tall . . . Last week there was a dream about the two of us driving somewhere together. I was driving because he had a horse in his lap.

11/12/06

Wet and leafless outside, early November view with the grass still green, the leaves all gone, the fields turning warm and gold . . . flares of light: the tamaracks on the hillside, a defiantly red little bush in our yard, a shock of tall weeds by the road glowing in sudden sunlight. It's not summer or winter or even autumn, as we think of these, but it is a quietly beautiful season all the same.

The Democratic victory in the midterm elections, the rain on the roof, the dog hairs on the sofa, the brain tumor in my head. As human beings we imagine in abstract enormities, but we live our lives in ordinariness. I can terrify myself with this brain tumor very easily. I know what to read: articles sent by well-meaning friends, postings on the Internet. I know who to call: two women in the area have had brain surgery within the past year and I've spoken with both of them. They're doing well but don't take the experience lightly. Or I can sit here by the fire that my beloved Nat has made in the living room, and read or work or lean back in this big leather armchair and look through my dirty windows at the November view. I could clean the windows, too, I suppose. But I might not.

11/20/06

Nat just walked through the room after a shower, wearing a shirt, his underwear, and a long string of dental floss draped around his neck.

"I'm feeling frivolous," he explained.

11/29/06

A week of holiday festivity and wedding planning combined, with Susannah and Jon [her fiancé] and Jon's parents visiting at the Mouse House [my mother's house], Nat's mother and Marek and Ben here— Lizzy and Dave [David Lindenberg, Lizzy's husband] were with his parents for Thanksgiving dinner, the rest of our crew in Montana, Colorado, and . . . ? Guatemala? Mexico?—too far away!

Thanksgiving with Nat's spectacular cooking along with [Nat's mother, Alice W. Tripp] Allie's mince pies and Jon's mother, Nancy's, cherry and pumpkin pies, cranberry sherbet from Lizzy and Susannah's Grandmother

*Brown's recipe—one of our traditions—along with sweet potato oranges
(Ansy's) and brussels sprouts, in memory of Ned [Perrin], who hated them.
Two more friends were here, Robin Berenbaum and her daughter Talia, so
there were lots of people around the table even without all the children.*

*One day after a morning when Nancy and I went wedding shopping
with Susannah, we gathered as many prospective in-laws as we could for
lunch at Anthony's Diner, including Richard, my dear silver-haired-and-
bearded ex-husband, handsome and elegant at this age. (He'd laugh to hear
himself described this way—"Who, me?" We had a cheery, greasy meal, then
Nat gave us all a tour of the restoration-in-progress at the Welcome Center /
Railroad Depot and gave some of us (Richard, Nancy, and her husband,
Andy) a tour of his Pullman car in its dark hideaway in the old train shed.*

*Everyone was impressed, and my ex-husband, who has spent years
(decades—two of them, anyway) recreating an old tavern on his farm in
Peacham brick by historic brick, was delighted: "Now I don't feel so crazy!"
he said with a grin as he clambered down from the Emperor. What is it with
me and men like this?*

December 3, 2006

This is my sweet Lizzy's birthday, and I love her so, so much.

December 4, 2006

*I woke from a dream that Nat and I were talking about my father as an
aviator. Nat was saying that it was true, as my mother had claimed, that you
could tell by looking at a plane in the air whether he was its pilot. (She
always said she could pick him out in the air.) In the dream, I said to my
husband, "Yes, he was a wonderful pilot," and Nat agreed, yes he was. In
the dream, I was thinking, or feeling—there were no words, but I know the
feeling: part pain, part comfort, one sharp and one gentle, surrounding the
other one—"At least we will always have that." "At least" says so much,
while saying nothing.*

December 5, 2006

The weeks go quickly and I go with them, moving along toward the surgery in mid-January, to remove my little meningioma—brain surgery sounds so huge and importantly drastic—so unlike me! It is always there, the apprehension and— yes—the fear. I dreamed about being with my kind neurosurgeon, Dr. Roberts, at a train station, with the train steaming and charging toward us—he reassuring me . . . and last night I was on a cliff with a clear and turquoise sea below, and swimmers. I asked how to get into that beautiful ocean—surely I didn't have to jump? It was so far down! How could anybody survive the drop? But they nodded, yes, I did, that was the only way to get into the water. They were very casual about it, but I thought no—I just can't.

December 10, 2006

It is Sunday morning, and so quiet that I don't know what to do with myself—Write? Christmas cards? Clean the house? There are many beds to make before Christmas. We have lots of people coming, we're delighted to report—I am getting excited.

December 14, 2006

Where am I? It is the middle of December and the sun is shining and the grass on the lawn outside my window is green. Beyond the lawn I can see that the surface of the smaller pond is still frozen, and the lilac branches outside my window have no sign of anything but wintry stillness, every bud well hidden, spring blooming only deep, deep, inside the tree.

December 28, 2006

Christmas has come and gone, and we're now in the tail of the holiday whirligig. We had Nat's mother and a bunch of the children and even the grand-twins, Phoebe and Stetson, all the way from Montana—a dozen of us around the living room, with tinsel and ribbons and wrapping paper, the tree alight and the fire crackling and glowing in the fireplace. (Where else would it be, Reeve? And "crackling"? There were flames and an occasional pop—does that count?) Marek and his father [Jerzy Sapieyevski] rolled in [last] Thursday night and filled the house with music—Jerzy played piano for Marek to sing "Erlkönig" and "La donna è mobile." How did I get a nephew who sings opera and plays banjo?

In the midst of everything the mailman staggered up the porch steps with two huge boxes from Thailand—one hundred full-sized paper parasols, for Susannah's wedding.

1/3/07

I don't believe in "rehearsing trouble," advice given to me years ago ("Don't rehearse trouble, Reeve!") by Helen Wallace, impossibly opinionated and delightfully talented pianist from Peacham. She was also a Christian Scientist, and she hated having people fuss about her health even in her nineties—of course SHE fussed about everything else!

On the other hand, we are talking about brain surgery. It happens in nineteen days—no, sixteen days; it happens on the 19th. What am I thinking? I'm not sure. I try not to anticipate too much, but I sometimes feel scared . . . and lonely.

1/5/07

There is some sense of a funneling and narrowing toward a point, which would be the brain surgery, but no sense of aftermath except in vague unpleasant apprehension: How much will my head ache? Will I be very low and depressed and feel removed from life? How long before I can write . . . drive . . . play tennis? But I can't imagine, can't plan, so I don't. Every day is sufficient unto itself, just this day.

Except for the dentists! My periodontist, whom I trust absolutely, thinks that I shouldn't risk any hint of gum infection before surgery, so he did a little "procedure" a week ago when I went for my checkup: three shots of novocaine in the vicinity of my upper front teeth, gums, and (it felt like) my nose, then scraping and "curettage" (sounds obstetrical but isn't). There were two post-op appointments scheduled, one now behind me and one to come. My local dentist, who plays saxophone in the town band and is married to a good friend of mine, also wants to see me, and I trust him, too. I don't think these are necessarily related, but good grief! Ansy used to talk about God Dentist—no matter what else is going on in your life, there's always something wrong with your teeth.

1/6/07

Susannah's birthday! I've sent flowers and a pretty little silken box with a silly silver pin in it—maybe a duck?—and a tiny mirror. I'll call today and might suggest not any more umbrellas (I meant "parasols") . . . but gently.

There is a feeling I get, in reference to the upcoming surgery, of being in some parallel universe, even while I'm going through these quiet days.

1/7/07

Twelve days to go, but who's counting? Me. One friend stopped by and left a pile of murder mysteries—she is so unobtrusive I didn't even know she'd been here—and another, bless the man, invited me to go with him on a bookstore prowl yesterday afternoon, first to Green Mountain Books in Lyndonville, with its glorious inventory of used books (and a few new ones), then to Galaxy Bookshop in Hardwick, another of my favorites. Our local bookstore, Boxcar & Caboose, is where I generally buy books, but we were going for a jaunt. He was looking for a gift for a scuba-diving niece. I was just having fun. The man behind the counter at the Hardwick store was wearing an unusual hat, something that might be in a portrait of Henry VIII (by Hans Holbein? Or am I in the wrong century?) but not so gaudy: no jewels, just a remarkable shape. He said they didn't have any scuba-ish books "for obvious reasons" (what are they? Vermonters hate the ocean? Don't believe in going underwater?). I kept looking at the hat. I had a lovely time, and when I got home Nat was cooking steak for dinner. People are being extremely kind to me. Should I worry?

1/10/07

Nat and I went to Dartmouth-Hitchcock yesterday to do preadmission things: filling out forms, talking to Sharon Morgan ARNP (nurse-practitioner, I believe), having blood work done and an EKG. I felt ridiculously pleased when I was told that my EKG was "beautiful—a textbook EKG." Sharon Morgan said that the blinking and eye sensitivity (to light, to smoke) may or may not be due to the tumor or the new medication. I told her that a couple of doctors had commented on the blinking but that Dr. Thompson felt it could be unrelated to the tumor. Sharon M. said that maybe some of this would change after surgery, but if not, had I considered seeing an eye doctor? I looked at her in surprise, then we both started laughing. No, I hadn't—an eye doctor? I thought everything in life was about the brain tumor . . . except, of course, for my teeth.

She said that there were some definite symptoms (of the brain tumor). My left big toe is "up" she explained, the way babies' toes are up—I don't really understand this—which makes sense if the tumor is on the right side of the brain. She also noted that one pupil seems more dilated than the other, but I forget which—would it be the left, again?

Tufts of snow on the lilac branches, snow on the lawn, snow on the road, a snowy roof on the barn. It looks as if there are only a few inches, but it's still snow. There has been so little of it this warm winter that some ski areas have closed and the surrounding hotels and businesses are in trouble. The dogs are chasing a gray squirrel—they won't catch it. Nat is in the shower. Ben is upstairs asleep. I'm here writing, trying not to blink.

1/11/07

Counting today there are eight more days (and two dentist appointments) before the surgery. I've been thinking about it and the image I have now is of ice fishing: they make a hole in a hard surface, then they fish something out from beneath. The ice-fishing holes are generally round, while the craniotomy hole as depicted in the Dartmouth-Hitchcock Medical Center handbook

Craniotomy: Understanding Your Care from Start to Finish *seems to be more or less square. There is a businesslike diagram on page three indicating each area to be exposed: "bone"; "underside of scalp flap"; "blood vessels"; "dura": "Under the skull is the tough covering of the brain, called the dura. The dura is cut and moved aside to expose the brain." Holy shit!*

There are some ambiguous sentences here, such as, "The bone that was removed will usually be put back in place at the end of the surgery." Or, "After anesthesia, the small air sacs in the lungs may collapse and have difficulty re-expanding" (page six). Side Effects May Include . . . And then there's the caution about the postoperative problems you might want to mention to your doctor, on page seven: "During this phase, it is important to note any changes in speech, arm and leg movements, and mental ability . . . Your family may need to help you with these observations." Yikes.

Well, I can't think about all of that this morning. I have a dentist appointment.

1/13/07

Nat has been working on a presurgery limerick:

> *While performing his first craniotomy*
> *The surgeon said "Ach! Oh, mein Gottamy!*
> *Underneath all that hair,*
> *There is nothing in there*
> *But a dream about pink hippopotamy!"*

1/14/07

Snow and more snow. After weeks of weather that felt like March—no snow, no cold, several ski areas unable to operate—now it's supposed to snow for two days nonstop. "Get used to that Weather Channel music," Nat warned me. He says that this time it really is the Mother of All Snowstorms. I giggle and roll my eyes. "You never listen to me," he says, aggrieved. "We could have three feet of snow!" I tell him it's true that I'm an expert in not-really-

listening from all those years with my father. You look them in the eyes, you nod at appropriate intervals, you even ask a pertinent question or two—but you're not really listening. Whether it's the Downfall of Civilization or the Mother of All Snowstorms, I can't listen to pronouncements in Capital Letters. I can't think that way. I think in lowercase.

Oh, I miss my sister. She knew how funny life is, even when you have a brain tumor—maybe even funnier with the brain tumor. What was it that Grace Paley wrote? "I am especially open to sadness and hilarity." That was about aging, not brain tumors, but it definitely applies.

Five days before the surgery including today. I don't feel fear or loneliness anymore. There is a kind of calm, and I spend my days planning, making lists, getting organized as if for a long journey, and maybe that's what it is. I think I need a new nightgown. Maybe I'll find one this week, if the Mother of All Snowstorms permits.

1/16/07

Some writers do their work in a powerful gulp, a whole book in a few months, nonstop, working days and nights. I'm the opposite kind of writer. I write very slowly, in dribbles and in multiple drafts over the years, and revise and revise and revise. If somebody didn't stop me (as an editor did once, very firmly: "That's enough, Reeve—it's time") I'd do it forever, like Galway Kinnell, who will revise a poem (change a word, fix punctuation, whatever seems required) even if it's in a book on a library shelf. I saw him do this myself, last year after a poetry reading.

1/17/07

Fourteen degrees below zero this morning. What happened to Global Warming? Ben is still here before this second semester starts, and will accompany Nat (and me) to the hospital on Friday; when I go in for the surgery he will be with his father. I am so touched, and so proud of him.

Yeah, I know . . . two days, today and tomorrow, then I get my brain unscrambled . . . and not a moment too soon.

1/19/07 4:00 A.M.

*Up at the pre-crack of dawn, we need to be at the hospital at 5:30 or 6:00 A.M. When he heard what time they wanted us there Nat said, "Think of it as a really bad charter flight." Ben's in the shower. Nat's making coffee (clear tea for me—no food at all allowed after midnight last night but clear liquids permitted until 5:00 A.M.). Two funny self-importances, both while bathing (no, while in the shower, but "both while bathing" is so alliterative). Yesterday I was pontificating, wetly, to an imaginary interviewer—I'm a Lindbergh, there's always an imaginary interviewer!—on the need to think of other human beings thoughtfully, not dismissively, always: to approach people personally rather than philosophically or politically or in any way with *ideas*—ideas make a veil, you can't see behind it—and today I imagined the doctors and nurses thinking what a great physical specimen I was—"and she's sixty-one!"— as I went into the operating room. Foolishness forever.*

1/22/07

It's over! The surgery happened on Friday and was completed by 1:30 P.M. We got to the hospital at 5:40 A.M. for preadmission and yet another MRI, but I think we went to the wrong door. We sat quietly at neurosurgery preadmissions while the MRI people were looking for us for half an hour. Nonetheless I was MRI'd and "prepped"—a little head shaving, the least of my concerns, but I bet I look funny under this cover-up-the-bandages hospital cap. (It needs a tassel—I made do with a rose.)

I liked the anesthesiologists, one of whom makes home-brewed beer, and said he'd bring me one for my recovery. I knew he was joking but liked the idea. The other one chatted and explained the process and then said, "I just slipped you a mickey," and was gone. I was gone, too. I think he patted my foot just before we both vanished. "That was nice," I said to Nat (I think I did, anyway), and the last thing I remember was Nat smiling at me.

Then it was done, about six hours later. I remember asking for the *anesthesiologist with the beer, but that's about it. Some delay in the recovery because of a heart arrhythmia. The doctors told Nat that was normal, but I was in the Special Care Unit overnight, not that I cared. It's just woozy and weird to have surgery and anesthetic, but you're not <u>there,</u> so you don't have to worry about anybody.*

Nat and Ben waited all day long. Thank God Ben was with his father. If I were alone waiting for Nat to come through brain surgery, wandering around that beautiful hospital all alone, it would be unbearable. I know this because now I've been both the person waiting for the loved one to come out of surgery (my first husband with his spinal surgery in New York long ago; my sister here at Dartmouth, surgery for the cancer, and we all hoped that would make it stop but it didn't even slow down), and now I'm the one coming out.

It's worse to wait. Nat came into the room the next morning, stood by the bed, and took my hand, then said, "Alice doesn't live here anymore." (I couldn't remember the reference, but I know it, it's from our teens or twenties, isn't it?) Then he began to cry. I know, I know.

Not that I didn't feel sick and strange and throbbing, not to mention nauseated—in fact that's as much as I want to mention about nauseated. But the IV painkillers took care of the pain for the first day, and after that I felt better enough to take Tylenol—plenty! Drugs are such a blessing. (Just say YES to drugs—at least after surgery.) It was astonishing to be able to rest, and quite well, after the operation, though with the IV and the little electric leg-squeezers (to prevent blood clots, I guess . . . a kind of perpetual massage) it was hard to change position, and my back ached. Big deal.

When Dr. Roberts came in the following day, he told me that everything had gone well with the surgery but that it was good to have removed the tumor. It was larger than expected and had pushed its way into several places from which it was tricky to remove it. This explains why the operation took twice as long as he'd expected. (He had thought about three hours.) I have an image of a starfish clinging to a coral reef, tentacles reaching inside cracks and crevices . . . brain coral?

Hospital World. Dr. Roberts advised me to start "walking around the Pod," even if I didn't feel like it, because this would help the recovery along. I didn't ask "What's the Pod?" because it had to be somewhere I could walk to and around while wheeling the IV apparatus, as indeed it was. First I walked with a nurse, the next time with all the children, who have gathered here in support. I walked around with my wires wheeling and my grown children tromping behind in their jackets and scarves and winter boots, grinning and talking. We got a little lost in the Pod, in fact. Nat came later and we did it again . . . Rock around the clock . . . Walk around the Pod.

What I mean by "Hospital World" is that the hospital is such an environment unto itself, with its own language and behaviors. Dartmouth-Hitchcock is an especially nice one in my experience (plenty!—not for myself but with others), full of light and characterized by the practical, personal, down-to-earth efficiency I associate with northern New England. From what I've now experienced and from all I heard previously, the neurosurgery team is superb. I was very happy to be there, if glad to leave on Sunday, a day earlier than expected. Surgery Friday, home on Sunday—I felt fine—amazing.

But it's still Hospital World. They're always "Taking Your Vitals" or "Temp," giving you "Meds," and asking the kinds of questions you wouldn't answer in any other context. "Do you still have your uterus?" a young nurse asked cheerfully while I was coming out of a dozing phase. I thought, Oh, God—did they start at the wrong end? but said yes, last time I looked I still had it. She explained that in order for the machine to measure liquid in the bladder accurately they have to know whether a woman has had a hysterectomy. If she has, they set the controls on "male." Hospital World.

1/26/07

An hour ago it was eighteen below zero, Nat says. I'm sitting in my chair in the living room with the fire going and with a crocheted fringed shawl wrapped around my shoulders, looking for Howard Mosher's address and

*the Vermont Country Store catalog—to tell Howard how much I love his
latest book,* On Kingdom Mountain, *which he sent me to read for possible
comment only I haven't quite finished it, and the catalog in the hope of
ordering some kind of very sturdy sofa slipcover affair to replace the one the
dogs ate.*

*Not bad, not bad at all. My ear is clearing today! There's still some
pulsing and noise in my head, but less of it. At first I had a steady, rhythmic
rushing in my ears, could feel the beat and the noise of it—loud—a little like
an earache except that it wasn't painful, just pulsing. Susannah said having
brain surgery so close to an ear must be like having a rock concert in your
head—maybe so.*

*I sit by the fire all day, or I lie on the bed in the sunroom and enjoy the
flowers people have sent. It's warm and quiet, with animals and people I
love coming in and out: Lizzy and Dave arrived again last night, and
friends visit or call daily. They talk, they smile, they pat me gently. I feel like
a very good dog.*

1/28/07

*Nat and I are both sleeping and snoozing a lot, though he works and cooks
and monitors the renovation work at the Railroad Depot, too. I sit and read
or write thank-you notes for flowers and get-well messages, using stationery
Nat made with a photo the kids took on the first night home from the
hospital, a week ago today. They dressed me in scarves and shawls and tied a
kind of pirate-cum-swami silk thing on my head, gave me a cutlass (what
was that thing?) and a kind of glittering disco ball we have that's the size of
a grapefruit, then took the picture. "Pirates of the Passumpsic," Nat
commented. (Madame Blavatsky? I thought.) When he sent one of these to
Sharon Francis, who runs the Connecticut River Joint Commissions, she
suggested alerting Homeland Security.*

2/4/07

Today my father would be 105 years old! I caught myself thinking of him so gratefully, deeply thankful for a brother in Europe I have come to know and love, and one who has sent so many thoughtful postsurgery messages—and so much chocolate!—heavens! Last night Nat dreamed about sea-sheep. They're exactly the same as regular sheep, only wetter. "They don't even taste fishy."

2/5/07

Wangari Maathai is being interviewed on the BBC about the effects of climate change on the African continent. At the very same time, CBS is doing a program on Superbowl hangovers (how to combat headache, nausea, muscle pain, and other ills caused by drinking too much alcohol while watching the game on Superbowl Sunday).

2/16/07

"Democracy is two wolves and a lamb voting on what to have for dinner. Liberty is a well-armed lamb contesting the vote." That's Benjamin Franklin, quoted by Bill Moyers, speaking at a meeting on media reform. Moyers's theme is "Censorship of knowledge by monopolization of the means of information." He's pretty clear that he thinks "Big Media" has sold out, literally, to moneyed interests, and feels there is only one response to this: "We have to tell the story ourselves." I have one question—who's "we"?

Another huge snow day on Thursday—five hundred schools across Vermont were shut down. Nat has been on the big green tractor, scooping and shoveling snow. He shoveled the walk and my path to the bird feeder and to his truck; says he'll shovel out my car tomorrow, but I can't drive for a few more weeks anyway. The dogs love this, romp belly-deep in the drifts. Yesterday Dolly [our newer dog] found a yellow chrysanthemum from one of my brain surgery bouquets in the compost heap, and pranced around with the flower in her teeth. Today she chased chickadees, thought she'd treed one, and got very excited. I'm not sure she understands wings.

3/11/07

Ben's twentieth birthday. We sent him books and love, and we had a nice birthday phone call. He's celebrating in NYC with some friends from Vermont, and Marek's taking him out for dinner. Twenty!

3/18/07

I'm here at the end of the table with Dotty the lamb in my lap. She was a triplet born on a terribly cold night, and must have gotten a little milk from the ewe at first, but weakened later, so we brought her in to the crate in the kitchen, and are feeding her with Sav-A-Lam milk replacer in a beer bottle. Nat laughs at me because I warm the solution, but sheep's milk comes warm from the ewe to the lamb, so why not ours?

3/25/07

Dotty went out with the other sheep, as of midday when Nat let all the other mothers and babies out of the birthing stalls and into the barnyard. I bring a bottle every four hours (daytime only!), and there's so much chaos with lambs and ewes that I don't think another lamb will notice, not in a way that will cause her harm. (What am I saying? Sheep? Notice? They don't have the brains for noticing.) Sheep Happens, as they say. For two weeks we've been deep in lambing, and trying hard to keep the vulnerable ones alive. We have fifteen lambs in the barnyard now out of nineteen babies born . . . The snow is melting, the sunshine brighter, and I feel as if I've woken from a two-week lamb-dream—or nightmare? A little of each . . .

4/11/07

I've learned something interesting about communication following brain surgery. I am so easily and so totally tired—it's like air going out of a balloon in one instant without warning—whoosh!—deflated. I like writing little notes or letters and sending them in the mail, but do as little e-mail as I can—it's exhausting. I don't know why. And except for family and local friends, I don't like using the phone, either, for the same reason. When the phone rings it's so shrill and insistent. "Answer me! Answer me!" Do I have to? No, I don't. The caller can leave a message. It's my telephone, after all.

And I can call back, or not. I can write a letter instead. I'm not sure it's polite to answer a phone call with a letter, but I now do this quite often. After phone calls I feel drained of energy, with the rush of personality in my ears, the eagerness, the urgency, the noise. I don't welcome this right now, so I respond on paper, in quietness.

5/3/07

Goldfinch on the lilac branch—bright yellow, like a lemon drop, then it's gone, replaced by a chickadee, who is like an old friend, less flashy but more familiar. My heart swells, and even though I don't know exactly what that means, I can feel it. I can <u>feel</u> it! I am filled with a sort of exhausted gratitude . . . Here it is, the world I love, in a chickadee alighting and bouncing on a branch, pecking at a bud, being itself as I watch it. Here we are, and one of us is crying . . . just a little bit, grateful to be, at least for this moment, absolutely and unquestionably alive.

10. The Good Lord
and the Details

When I was a writer in my midtwenties, just beginning to think about trying to publish something I had written, I sought advice from my mother's editor, who was also our close family friend, Helen Wolff. Mrs. Wolff, of Helen and Kurt Wolff Books, had become a legend in the publishing business in this country since the time she and her husband fled the Nazis and left their publishing work in Vienna during the Second World War. Even when I first met her as a child, she was an important figure in the literary world.

I didn't know Mrs. Wolff's reputation when I first met her, probably because I was young and had no interest in this kind of information. I knew her only as the quiet woman with the pleasant voice and funny accent, who wore very soft, comfortable-looking brown or gray suits and came frequently to have tea with my mother.

She visited us in the old house in Connecticut during the years I was growing up, and then she visited in the newer, smaller house my parents had built later on the same property, after their five children had grown up and left home. During the earlier visits she was often accompanied by her husband, a tall, thin man whose face I remember for its long boniness, kind smile, and bright, amused eyes that looked directly down into mine. He died when I was still in my teens, and I continue to wish I had known him longer. Even as a child I could tell that in Kurt Wolff there were all the qualities I love best in people: compassion, intelligence, humor, and joy.

After his death Mrs. Wolff spoke of her husband often, as though they continued to be the working team that had given their name and spirit to the books they published, first at Pantheon and then at Harcourt, and in a sense this was absolutely true. I remember that she pronounced his name with a rich lingering roundness that made the word something between "curt" and "court," but much more melodious because of the affection in her voice.

Helen Wolff had a low, even voice, and she chuckled deeply when she was amused. It was always good to be in her company, but there were two qualities above all others that drew me to Mrs. Wolff. She treated children exactly as she treated adults, and she was polite to animals.

Many of our visitors, seeing that we had a dog, entered the house with loud voices and waving hands, making a noisy fuss over him. This kind of behavior just caused the poor dog to slink off into a corner and stay there until the visitors left. Helen Wolff came in without commotion and then sat quietly and drank her tea, like the well-behaved guest that she was. The dog came over to greet her, eventually, sniffing her hand and wagging his tail, probably grateful for her good manners. She told me once that she felt it was better to let animals or children come to her, if they wished to, rather than the other way around.

Like the dog, I came to her, too, shyly at first and then with more confidence as the years passed. I shared a little of myself at the beginning of our friendship by answering her polite inquiries about school activities and interests. Then, as I grew older, I wrote to her about my writing. Her replies were always both prompt and thoughtful, and I read her letters with surprised pleasure. She seemed to understand not only what I wanted to say, sometimes even better than I did, but also who I was. She did not behave as if my seeking her out was an imposition, or even a distraction from the other, more important things in her life, as it surely was.

Later still, when I came to her as an unpublished writer of twenty-five, she responded with the same respect she had shown to the ten-year-old at the tea table in Connecticut. The only real difference in our relationship was that now I knew who *she* was. I was aware that she had worked not only with my mother, but also with Günter Grass and Boris Pasternak and Iris Origo and with countless others whose work impressed me tremendously, even when, as in the case of Günter Grass, I didn't understand it.

I was tremendously impressed, but I was also young and eager. Where should I attempt to publish my work? I asked Helen Wolff.

My "work" at that time consisted of one or two pieces of short fiction drawn largely from my own experience and thinly disguised in short-story form. Mrs. Wolff did not tell me where to publish these, exactly, but she did ask me if I would send them to her to read. I was delighted, and I did so. After reading the stories, she sent them back with some helpful comments and the name of an agent she liked very much, Rhoda Weyr, whom she suggested I contact. I got in touch with Rhoda, and I, too, liked her very much, especially because she loved Helen Wolff almost as much as I did.

Rhoda and I worked together in friendship and in mutual understanding for more than twenty years, until her recent retirement. The only real disagreement between us I can remember had to do with mud and cows. She just didn't see why these two elements figured so prominently in my writing about Vermont. She lived in Brooklyn, New York, and did not spend a lot of time in the country. I tried to explain the situation here, and she tried to understand me. I think she must have come to do so, finally, because when Rhoda retired from her work as a literary agent, she moved to Maine. I'll bet she has encountered as much mud and as many cows there as I have here in Vermont.

Along with the name of this excellent agent, Helen Wolff also gave me some very good advice about writing. Much of this came in conversations we had over the course of the years as well as in the letters. I suspect my memory may have trimmed it all to fit my own experience, but I think of Mrs. Wolff's combined wisdom as three teachings, principles that have guided me through my work, and to a great extent through my life as well.

The first piece of advice was this: if you are a writer, the most important thing you can do is to write. Just write. Go ahead and do it. It doesn't matter that you don't know where the writing will lead. The practice of writing itself will be much more useful to you than your certainties, or your uncertainties, about the direction and purpose of the work. Whether you think you know where you are going with it or not, keep on writing, and write just as regularly as you can. Ultimately, if you keep at it, the writing itself will take you where you need to go.

Many contemporary authors of books on writing, from Natalie Goldberg *(Writing Down the Bones)* to William Zinsser *(On Writing Well)*, will say the same thing. If you want to write, you have to write.

It seems obvious enough, but to follow this advice takes courage. For one thing, writing on a regular basis doesn't necessarily work for everybody, though it does work for me. Some people really and truly need to write *irregularly,* as inspiration hits. I don't know how they do it, frankly, but I have several writer friends who work this way. They seem to go fallow for a while, like a farmer's field, writing nothing at all. Then they produce reams of material in a short space of time, and they come up with just as much good writing as the people who write slowly, like me. I move along at the pace of the turtles I love; therefore I try for as much regularity as I can muster, to cover the ground I know I have to travel.

Writing regularly also means stepping out into the unknown again and again. It is only human nature—my nature, certainly—to step right back again, or to step aside, step around, do a two-step, whatever I can do to keep away from the void that yawns before me every time I pick up pen and paper, or turn on the computer, to write. If I were advising a young writer today as Helen Wolff once advised me, I'd say, "Be aware that you are stepping into the void every time you sit down to write. I am aware of this, too. I don't like it, either. Do it anyway."

Write sporadically if you must, write only a few paragraphs, or a few sentences, even a few words at a time if that's all you can get down on paper. Don't ever wait for "inspiration." Inspiration may come and is a great blessing if it does, but don't hold back from writing until it arrives. Don't hold back, either, because you think you have to have everything planned out ahead of time. Plans and outlines can be helpful, but if planning becomes too important, the completion of a plan may be as far as you get with your work. You may never take the plunge into the messy, disorganized, unpredictable business of writing, sentence after sentence and paragraph upon paragraph. That's where the real work gets done.

Another thing about planning is that your writing may go off in a completely different direction from your plan's indicated path. If this happens, in my opinion you must let it go, and go with it. The work will still need your guidance and your skill, but it must not be stifled by fear of abandoning a plan. Writing has its own plans, and its own sense of direction, too. In my experience, it's best to follow where it takes you, and the way to follow is to keep on writing.

I think I resist Helen Wolff's first piece of advice every day of my writing life, but nonetheless I believe what she told me. If you want to be a writer, write. Don't talk about it, do it. Start right now, and write a little, and then stop if you have to (or if you can!). Then, soon, do it again. And again. Pretty soon writing will become a part of your daily life, and you'll be surprised at what happens next.

I have had to rely heavily on trickery, subterfuge, and self-deception for years, just to keep myself writing regularly. I fight a constant battle with my own laziness and distractibility, and I have come up with countless gimmicks to keep myself writing—writing *anything*—on a regular basis. It isn't easy. As procrastination and avoidance of writerly responsibilities go, I'm the toughest case I know.

There is always something I think I should be doing that is much more urgent and immediate than my real (i.e., writing) work. Urgencies and immediacies can range from responding to the needs of family members to listening to the joys and woes of friends to volunteering on committees for really good causes . . . right down to sorting the laundry and, if I'm really desperate, cleaning out the refrigerator. This is a perfect procrastination device because when it's over I am both exhausted and virtuous: too tired to write but not feeling one bit guilty. I cleaned the refrigerator!

Knowing me as I do, I try to work with myself in a positive way, and to turn my writerly failings into assets. I avoid writing by writing. If I am running away from an article or a book review or—ahem—a chapter for a new book, I eagerly start to work on an unfinished poem for a children's book, or even an unbegun one. Today, for instance, while sitting in the quiet little Writer's Room, a space set aside for people like me in our local library, and while knowing that I absolutely need to be working on my book, I've been composing a poem about Homer, the librarian's cat.

Homer disappeared for several weeks this past summer, upsetting the whole library community. Everybody loved Homer, a stray who came to live with Glo, our equally beloved children's librarian. He was a favorite in the neighborhood. One day he came to the library when Glo was reading the younger children some books about cats. For some reason, Homer shot out the door suddenly, and was not seen again for weeks and weeks. Everybody was looking for him, all around the building and all around the town. The people who worked in the town offices and the fire department, on the north side of the library, were watching for Homer, and the people who worked at the post office, on the south side, were looking for him, too. Children and their families put posters up, everyone told their friends. It was an intense time. Then, just as suddenly, Homer turned up again, to the delight of all.

I was asked to write something to celebrate Homer's adventures and his return—in effect, Homer's Odyssey. (That's what I get for hanging out with librarians.) Maybe we will find a local artist to illustrate the work, and make a poster, with copies for all the children who come to the library. Who knows? I changed the story quite a bit, but Homer is still the hero, and he will remain the central character through all the revised versions I know I'll write. (I always do.) This is it, so far:

> *Homer was a house cat*
> *Homer didn't roam*
> *Glo went to the library*
> *Homer stayed home.*
>
> *Glo read to the children*
> *Sitting in her lap*
> *Children took their books home*
> *Homer took a nap.*

Homer was a quiet cat
He did not hunt at all
If Homer heard a bird, he purred,
Mice played with his ball.

It needs work, I know. I'm just setting the scene, here, and establishing character traits. The rest of the story will come later, probably just about the time I get stuck in the next chapter of this book.

Another procrastination device, subtly subversive in my case, is to write in a journal. I do this, if not daily then quite regularly. If I have a deadline for another writing project, I sometimes write in my journal for hours at a time. This is self-deceptive procrastination, fueled by a notion lurking somewhere at the back of my brain that journal writing is not the same thing as Writing.

Much of my published work has come directly from my journals, but journal writing never seemed important to me in a literary way. I called it "just writing in my diary" for years, and only recently learned I could upgrade the whole experience by calling my diary a "journal," and the writing I do in it "journaling." There are workshops, books, classes taught in colleges on "journaling" now, but to me it has always felt like playing hooky from the real thing. If I'm not writing in my office on the computer, or not writing on my usual paper with my usual pen somewhere in my house or in the library's Writer's Room, then I think it doesn't count.

I get a lot of work done this way, avoiding Writing by writing, and lately I've learned another, even more self-subverting trick. I keep any ongoing writing project, like this book, in exactly the same place where I write letters, pay bills, and keep my diary—no, my *journal*. That is the informal, cluttered, not-Writing place at one end of the dining room table. We can barely dine here, in fact, because Nat and I both work at this table, one of us at one end and one at the other, spreading our letters and books and papers all over it.

We each have an official "office" space, too. His is downstairs, a small comfortable cave of a room between the woodshed and the back hallway and laundry area. He has a row of filing cabinets along one wall, and two tables that provide an L-shaped work surface along another two walls. One surface holds his computer and his printer along with associated papers and possessions. Another has his electric typewriter, which he still uses for a number of tasks, including typing his own journal. The typed journal is mostly a carefully kept record of the weather and natural events around the farm, he says, and it sits on a table overflowing with books and papers, a nest that surrounds him when he sits there.

My office is upstairs. It is a room full of light just under the eaves, with a long table that fits perfectly in the space made for the dormer window. On the floor are boxes and boxes of books: mine, my mother's, my sister's, always a few treasures from used-book stores, often a pile that I think I'll give away or send to somebody, but haven't gotten around to yet. When I work at the computer, I look out through the windows and can see across the field, past the apple trees to the pond and to the spot at the far edge where my mother's former writing house now sits, looking back at me. After her death it was brought here on a flatbed truck all the way from Connecticut, and despite the uprooting it looks very comfortable here in Vermont. I sometimes wonder if this is where it came from to begin with.

My mother's old writing house is a converted toolshed my parents bought years ago in one piece and painted blue-gray, with white trim around the windows and red shutters. It has a wooden door of a style that I remember as "Dutch." The top and bottom halves of the door can be opened separately. If someone opens that door as a whole, these days, and enters the house, they will see my mother's desk and chair still sitting against one wall by the window overlooking the pond, and a cushioned, cotlike sofa against the opposite wall, where she used to stretch out and rest sometimes. There are a few of her other possessions left, too: a Swiss dishtowel in a cheerful print, pinned to a wall with ancient thumbtacks; a piece of gray and tangled driftwood tied to a beam with a piece of string. But now there are canoe paddles on the floor as well, and a double-bladed paddle for the kayak Nat and I won in a charity lottery, and sometimes a half-inflated rubber raft one of our children used during a summer visit. It feels as if the house is gently reverting to its original purpose. I don't think my mother would have minded at all.

What I remember mainly about my mother's writing house, back in Connecticut during the time I was growing up, was that it was a place where I was not supposed to disturb my mother if she was working there. I remember, too, that she did not always work there. She sometimes worked at the big desk in the living room that had once been her father's, and she sometimes worked at the little writing desk in her bedroom. She may have done most of her writing in the writing house, I really don't remember, but I do know that it was not the only place where she wrote. Moreover, I'm willing to bet that the little house became a Writing Place for her, and the idea of going there was a hindrance to her work at times, just as being there and working was a help at other times.

I think that having a designated Writing Place may be a little like having a piece of exercise equipment in your home. You think that because you have the machinery right there with you, every day, and you know how to use it, you'll use it all the time. You'll exercise much more often than you would if you went to the gym once or twice a week. It stands to reason. Yet I am told that some of the most common items in yard sales are home exercise machines, lightly used. I'm not at all surprised.

I'd say that it is good to have a quiet place to work, and it is also good not to work there, but somewhere else—whether at one end of the dining room table, or sitting in an armchair by the fireplace, or even away from all the usual writing spots entirely. I carry many pens and at least one cheap spiral notebook with me wherever I go, on the theory that if an idea should come to me while I'm traveling, I can write it down for future use. Some people travel with laptop computers and other electronic devices for the same reason, but I'm still happiest carrying a notebook. Sometimes I even write something in it.

I was waiting for my son at the Boston airport in August, for instance, absentmindedly watching the people who came through the waiting area. For one brief moment, I thought I caught a glimpse of someone I knew very well, someone I loved but had not seen for a long time. Just after the first flash of heartwarming recognition, just before I rose from my seat to call out a greeting, I realized that I was mistaken. The person I thought I'd seen could not possibly be in Boston, because he was no longer on this earth. In my absentmindedness I had resurrected a dear, dead friend, and not for the first time, either. There is something about airports and train stations, those places of mass movement where people pass by again and again, that makes it seem possible to see anybody you have ever known, living or dead . . . almost.

I took out my notebook and wrote about the experience, the combined joy and pain of it, while these feelings were, so to speak, still warm. I felt a little apologetic as I wrote, wondering whether "capturing" such feelings was such a good thing. Maybe it was better just to feel them, and let them go. But I am a writer, apologetic or not, so I wrote.

Most often, when I fish these notebooks out of my handbag to see what I have written in them, I find travel schedules, grocery lists, notes from meetings, and directions to bookstores, schools, or libraries where I've been asked to speak. Sometimes I find quotations or excerpts from other writers, words that seem piercingly appropriate at a particular moment in time. I copied this not long ago from Azar Nafisi's book *Reading Lolita in Tehran*. The author is describing her changed sense of herself after the Islamic fundamentalists came to power in Iran:

> I had not realized how far the routines of one's life create the illusion of stability. . . . Now that I could not wear what I would normally wear, walk in the streets to the beat of my own body, shout if I wanted to or pat a male colleague on the back on the spur of the moment, now that all of this was illegal, I felt light and fictional, as if I were walking on air, as if I had been written into being and then erased in one quick swipe.

I copied the paragraph because it was as beautifully written as it was frightening. Nafisi's words make me aware of the conditions that many writers around the world have to live with every day. Her words remind me that these writers manage to keep writing anyway. They bear witness to their experience, right down to their own threatened bodies walking down their own streets in their own cities, alive to the possibility of being "erased in one quick swipe" in one way or another, at any moment. If for no other reason, I want to keep on writing because they do.

The second piece of advice Mrs. Wolff gave me, and this was in one of her letters, addressed the importance of having confidence in one's own written words. If you have written something clearly, she said, have the good sense to leave it alone. Don't keep fussing at it in the sentences and paragraphs that follow, "like a housewife plumping pillows."

I am smiling as I set her words down here, "like a housewife plumping pillows." I can see them in her handwriting just as she wrote them, in her careful European script. And they were so true! I am far from being a tidy housewife, in or out of my writing life, but this phrase describes me perfectly as a writer, then and now, so I have to smile. If I don't feel sure I have written something the way I want it to be, I do fuss with it over and over, tweaking and poking and repeating myself, not sure I've finished the job. I surround a simple statement with parentheses, and appositives, and the inept, timid phrases "it was as if," and "in other words." What does that mean, anyway? *What* "other words"? What's wrong with the original words? Those very words, "in other words," often mean trouble.

When I become Helen Wolff's fussy housewife, I know that my writing is weak, and I must face another realization, too: I probably need to cut words from whatever I'm working on, maybe a whole lot of words. I know this because it has become painfully clear to me over time that I can almost always strengthen what I have written by cutting words, almost never by adding them. It is humiliating, but it is true.

The most useful thing I ever learned in a book about writing, by far, is still from Strunk and White's 1957 classic, *The Elements of Style*. It comes in Chapter II, "Elementary Principles of Composition," lesson 13, "Omit needless words." Along with my favorite teachings by the noble mouse in *Stuart Little* (like "Absolutely no being mean") and the canny observations of the writer of rural essays (like "One of the most time-consuming things is to have an enemy"), surely one of E. B. White's greatest gifts (and surely Mr. Strunk's greatest gift) to literature is this phrase, "Omit needless words." I suppose there are exceptions, but nine times out of ten, in writing anything at all, you're in good shape if you do and in bad shape if you don't. It's as simple as that.

The final piece of advice Mrs. Wolff gave me had to do with

abstractions and details. Wherever possible, Mrs. Wolff cautioned, a good writer should avoid the former in favor of the latter.

"Remember what Flaubert said to De Maupassant," she wrote to me, "Le Bon Dieu est dans les détails" (the Good Lord is in the details).

"Remember"? I was so flattered that she thought I'd even heard of Flaubert and De Maupassant that I pretended to know exactly what she was talking about, and after thinking about it, I almost did.

"The Good Lord is in the details." This statement sometimes has been attributed to Mies van der Rohe and others, but I bet they, too, got it from Flaubert, if Mrs. Wolff did.

What details? You may ask yourself this question, because I certainly did. In fact I still do. There are details and there are details. Even in Flaubert's own *Madame Bovary,* a book about a love affair, quite tame by modern standards, there are one or two details from which a reader might wish to be spared. A century after it was written, we had what was then called a "Sexual Revolution," and whatever else this may have done for the world, it released volumes of graphically detailed material upon the unsuspecting reading public. I don't think this was what Flaubert or Mrs. Wolff had in mind.

Details, in the wrong hands, are about as tedious as anything else on earth. We have all heard the speaker who puts an audience to sleep by droning on at length about a specialized area of knowledge. I once attended a lecture in which a renowned scientist, an otherwise charming man, listed the medicinal properties of tropical plants for a full hour, alphabetically. I started to doze a little at "asthma," and woke up with a start at "jock itch."

I don't think that the details of writing or of speaking, either, need to be titillating on the one hand, or tedious on the other. I think that details on the written page need to be there for their own interesting sake, and to hold a place for all that is real in our lives, minute by minute and molecule by molecule.

Details represent our only tangible truth, don't they? I may believe that I live in my thoughts and feelings, hoping wistfully for mostly "good" ones—open-mindedness, ethical consideration, compassion, and delight, knowing that some will be more difficult—fear, rage, grief, and despair. But how much more truly I live in the details of my body and its functions. How much more truly I live in the details of my day.

Here are the rumpled sheets on the bed in the morning, here is the frost on the windowpane. Here are the steep wooden stairs, creaking as my husband descends with the dog bounding ahead of him. Here is the hiss of the kettle, boiling water for coffee, and the slam of the door as the dog goes outside, and another when she comes in again. Here is the crisp winter air against my face when I leave the warm house, here the sound and feel of grit in the dirt driveway under my shoes as I walk to the car. Here is the familiar roar of the engine starting, the sights and sounds of the drive along our dirt road and down the hill, past mailboxes and neighbors' farmhouses, stands of pine and open fields. Here is the paved road to St. Johnsbury and the library, where I have come to work on this book.

Or else there are the details of working at home, another day, upstairs in my office, with my cluttered desk and the computer in front of me, and books at my back. Here I am surrounded by books, in fact, on shelves and in boxes, my own books and books by my family members and books by other writers. I am surrounded, too, by my collection of personal treasures, details of the heart: photographs, pictures on the wall, stones and seashells, paperweights made by young children, tokens and remembrances all around me. In these details, too, I live.

I remember so well the way my mother and Helen Wolff sat

together on the sofa, Mrs. Wolff in her suit and my mother in another one, hers probably in a shade of pink or lavender. Or maybe my mother wore pants ("trousers," she called them) and a pink blouse with a scarf or a pin at the neck. Each woman held her knees together neatly, as women had been trained to do in that era, and each sat slightly at an angle to her friend. Knees pointed toward knees, making conversation easier and silence more intimate.

I can see the china teapot and the teacups, on a wooden tray sitting on a table just in front of the two women, with another bright-patterned Swiss linen towel spread beneath the china. The cups were bone china, I believe, white and almost translucent, and very light to hold, even when filled with tea and milk and sugar, or tea with a slice of lemon floating on top. The table was low and dark and very heavy, a solid rectangle of old oak that ran almost the whole length of the small sofa, but not quite. A chain of small interlocked and pointed arches had been carved on the outside of the raised rim framing the four sides, so the table itself looked like a kind of Celtic tray table, built for massive Saxons in drafty medieval halls. I learned only recently that it was originally a bench, with an embroidered cushion made to sit neatly inside the raised rim. I figured this out after finding the cushion in a closet in my mother's house sometime after her death. She must have decided long ago that this piece of furniture made a better table than a bench, and I agree with her.

That same table is now in our living room, in front of the fireplace. Last night I sat by the fire talking with my husband, watching the flames move and the coals glow. I saw the reflection of light on the dark wood of my mother's tea table, and I thought of my mother and Helen Wolff sitting together and talking, knees to knees, writer to editor, friend to friend. They are both with me this morning, in every detail I can still remember, and in every word I write.

11. Noel Perrin and the DMV

Sometimes when a good friend dies it takes a long time before you really feel it. There is shock and sadness right away, of course, and there is an absence like a hole in the air where something should be, but isn't. You may drive past the person's house and find yourself choking back the familiar thought, *That's where my friend lives,* because you know this is not true, not anymore. Still, you don't *really* feel the death, because it is impossible to comprehend right away that all the little things you knew and loved about the person have vanished from your life forever. As in the old song, it is a matter of "the way you wear your hat, the way you sip your tea," or laugh, or walk, or stand, or open the door, or answer the telephone, or write a letter.

For me there is always a numb, unsettled time after a death, a period when, as Emily Dickinson wrote, "a formal feeling comes / The nerves sit ceremonious, like tombs." Feeling is suspended because everything about the person has been so disrupted by the one huge truth of their death, which carries with it not only a "formal feeling," but also formalities. There are funerals and tributes and "celebrations of life," all gatherings of people who are upset by this loss. It is a great comfort to be with others who share one's grief, but there is so much happening that, for me, the person who died may get lost, again, in the commotion.

Later on, when things quiet down, my friend usually comes back. I don't mean this in any supernatural way. Nobody has yet appeared to me in the form of a ghost or an angel, though I'm still waiting. Often the person just stops by for a visit in the form of some tangible reminder so characteristic of him or her that all my feelings return in a flood. When this happens I am always grateful.

The death I am thinking about now is that of my dear friend and former brother-in-law, Noel Perrin. He was a well-known American writer and staunch environmentalist, a Dartmouth professor, a part-time farmer, and a prominent and widely loved Vermont citizen. He died on November 21, 2004, at his home in Thetford, at the age of seventy-seven. He visited me the following spring, courtesy of the Vermont Department of Motor Vehicles.

Ned Perrin was diagnosed in 2002 with Shy-Drager syndrome, a rare and, as he described it, "particularly nasty" form of Parkinson's disease. In a letter addressed to friends, colleagues, and relatives in September of that year, Ned wrote that "one of the consequences of Parkinson's is a drop in writing ability. Both the physical act (one's handwriting gets tinier and tinier, even within a single word) and the verbal fluency."

The letter was the first item in a yellow folder marked in pencil on the tab "VT DMV 2003," which surfaced some months after Ned's death. My husband was the executor for his estate, and the folder had been left on our dining room table. Curious, I took a look inside. I saw a stack of papers an inch thick, mostly correspondence between Ned and various representatives of the Vermont Agency of Transportation. At the very back there are a few insurance forms and a couple of accident reports.

Accident reports. Ah, yes. I remember Ned's accidents. To be fair, one of the two reports here concerns a friend who borrowed

Ned's truck on an icy day and ran into trouble, and ultimately a tree. The other report was filed by Ned himself, after his hybrid Toyota Prius left Route 5 on a perfectly clear day in July and tangled with a barbed-wire fence.

I happen to know that this was not Ned's first or his last automobile accident, but it is the only one reported in the file. The majority of the papers in the yellow folder deal not with any accident in particular, but with the suspension of Ned's license by the state of Vermont in 2002 and his efforts to reverse that suspension in 2003.

None of these documents, and nothing in my memory either, can change my opinion of the driving skills of my late friend and all-time favorite absentminded professor. His vehicular adventures are legendary.

I heard from my nephew, for instance, about Ned driving him up the ramp onto Interstate 95 at 15 mph, oblivious to the trucks roaring up and honking behind him as they sped south from the Canadian border. Ned did not seem to notice the trucks, my nephew told me, because at the time he was busy advancing his theory that every highway in this country should maintain a special lane for horses and buggies.

I was Ned's passenger myself on another occasion when he drove slowly, and, astonishingly, without even pausing once, through every single stop sign on Railroad Street in St. Johnsbury on the way to breakfast at a local diner one Sunday morning.

It is because of Ned that I know it is not necessary to have a driver's license to operate a tractor in the state of Vermont. The reason I know this is that Ned's wife, Sara Coburn, has told us about the time following his license suspension when Ned drove his tractor along a local road toward the tractor dealership for needed repairs. She was following in the car.

Before they arrived at the dealership, Ned inadvertently let the cutter bar (the attachment used for mowing hayfields) down behind him. Despite Sara's desperate honking of her horn and blinking of her lights as she followed the tractor, the cutter bar sliced off the roof of a pickup truck parked along the road as if it were the top of a hard-boiled egg.

Though there is little in the folder to support his driving expertise, Ned's other qualities are here in force: intelligence, generosity, patience, good manners, charm, persistence, "verbal fluency" (Parkinson's notwithstanding), and, above all else, courage.

Immediately following the September letter to friends about his deteriorating condition, there are seven typed notices in the folder, each addressed to Noel Perrin from the commissioner of motor vehicles. Two of them are in capital letters, as in "REFERRING TO OUR SUSPENSION/REVOCATION/DISQUALIFICATION DATED 12/25/02." None of the seven shows much sign of having been touched by a human hand. In fact, not one is signed by the commissioner or by anybody else. Each tells its own tale.

Form #1, confusingly dated 12/16/02 while referring to the above notice of 12/25/02, states that the "Suspension/Revocation/Disqualification" of Ned's license has been canceled and removed from the record.

That's one license suspension and one cancellation of the suspension.

Form #2, also dated December 16, lets it be known that Ned's Driver Eyesight Evaluation Form has been received, and that a written and driving test has been scheduled for him on Thursday, January 23, 2003. They know he can see, now they want to see if he can drive.

There is a reasonable-looking cautionary sentence about halfway down the page on Form #2. "You must bring a vehicle in proper mechanical condition that is suitable for you to use to take the driving test."

The words resonate ominously with me when I read them

only because I know about the previous summer's adventure involving Ned, the Prius, and the barbed-wire fence. Long before I ever saw this folder, my husband visited Ned and Sara at the farm in Thetford one fall day not too long after the accident. Nat told me that the Prius looked as if it had been driven from Thetford to St. Johnsbury through the woods and then beaten with chains. How was it ever made "suitable" for the driving test?

As it turned out there was a more significant sentence in Form #2, further down: "If you fail to appear for the scheduled exam, your license will be suspended." I don't know why, but he did, and it was.

Form #3, dated February 5, detailing this second suspension and its consequences, makes me angry with the Motor Vehicles Department. Why all caps? Hasn't the DMV heard of *italics,* for heaven's sake?

Why blare to the world that Ned's license "AND/OR PRIVILEGE OF OPERATING ANY MOTOR VEHICLE IN THE STATE OF VERMONT IS HEREBY SUSPENDED EFFECTIVE FEBRUARY 2003, INDEFINITELY, TO REMAIN IN EFFECT UNTIL SUCH TIME AS YOU RECEIVE PROPER NOTICE, FROM THIS DEPARTMENT, OF YOUR REINSTATEMENT . . . YOU SHALL NOT, UNDER ANY CIRCUMSTANCES, EVEN WHEN ACCOMPANIED BY A LICENSED DRIVER, OPERATE OR ATTEMPT TO OPERATE A MOTOR VEHICLE IN VERMONT . . ."

Why underline "EVEN"? It just seems so MEAN!

Form #4, dated February 10, is an improvement: "As requested, we have scheduled you another appointment."

Form #5, not too long afterward, is just another "SUSPENSION/REVOCATION/DISQUALIFICATION HAS BEEN SUSPENDED AND REMOVED FROM THE RECORD," just like the other one. We now have two suspensions and two cancellations of suspensions.

Form #6, dated March 11, is not in caps, and is almost polite. (About time!) It begins, "Thank you for appearing recently for the written test." Alas, the next line breaks my heart, even in lowercase. "Since you failed the written test, it will be necessary to suspend your privilege to operate in Vermont."

The DMV evidently did not know with whom they were dealing. Not even this formidable bureaucracy could suspend Noel Perrin's "privilege to operate in Vermont." They could merely suspend his right to operate a motor vehicle in Vermont, and even that took some doing.

Form #7 is the same mean-spirited suspension notice. It is dated March 14 but is exactly like the one of February 5, including "EVEN" and all the rest of it. I turned it over quickly.

After the seven forms comes a personal letter. It is dated March 22, 2003, and addressed to the commissioner of motor vehicles. It was written on the Dartmouth College Environmental Studies Program letterhead, and signed by Professor Noel Perrin.

It is more of a memo than a letter, really, but it was obviously written by a gentleman, not a machine. It was written *on* a machine, not a computer but a typewriter. Ned did have a computer, but he used it only for sending e-mail messages, which he called "blitzes" for some reason. Everything else he wrote by hand or on a typewriter, like this memo.

It is brief:

> *To the Commissioner of Motor Vehicles:*
> *Request for hearing on the suspension of my driver's license.*
> *I hereby request a hearing in this matter.*

"I hereby request" is good, isn't it? I like that little echo of a rhyme in the last line, with "hereby" and "hearing." The whole communication has a great and poetic dignity.

Note that this letter or memo, whichever it is, was written a good six months after the first letter in the folder, in which Ned warned friends and colleagues of his "drop in writing ability." Six days later, on March 28, he sent another letter, as follows:

Thetford Center, VT 05075
March 28, 2003

To The DMV:

On March 14th the DMV sent me a letter saying that my license is to be suspended, effective April 3rd. The letter also said that I could request a hearing, if I made the request in writing and within 15 days.

On March 22nd I did make that request in writing. A copy is enclosed.

So, what am I writing you about now? I just want to be sure that my request of March 22nd did arrive safely at the Policy and Hearing Section. I expect it did. But I'm a worrier, and I just want to be sure.

I enclose a self-addressed envelope.

Sincerely,
Noel Perrin

If you would just say something like "We got it," I'd be a happy man.

This letter has been folded once vertically and three times horizontally, as if it had been mailed away in a standard business envelope and mailed back again in a much smaller one. There is an official notice stamped across the top of the page at a tipsy angle. If I tilt my head to the side, I can read it:

RECEIVED
March 31, 2003
Policy-Hearing Section
Agency of Transportation

Miraculously, there is also a handwritten note at the bottom of the page, printed cheerfully in bright red pen. "Yes, we got it, and a letter went out in today's mail." The note is not signed, exactly, but it is initialed, I think, at the end of the message. The mark looks deliberate, anyway, and it resembles a little red flower. I can tell that by March of 2003, Ned was beginning to get to these people, and I'm not surprised. He always did.

True enough a real letter follows acknowledging Ned's request for a hearing and declaring his license suspension to be "held in abeyance pending a hearing on the matter." The license suspension, Ned's third, has been suspended a third time.

The letter is addressed politely, "Dear Mr. Perrin," and is signed by Gordon P. Currier, AOT Policy and Hearings Chief. Mr. Currier's name shows up frequently in the exchanges of March and April of 2003. There is a March 1 notice scheduling a hearing for April 11 by telephone. I have never before heard of a hearing by telephone, but apparently they exist, and Ned was going to get one. There is an April 3 letter explaining the terms of the hearing and the conditions of the license suspension, and restating Ned's arguments against the suspension:

You not only teach Environmental Studies at Dartmouth College but also specifically focus on the subject of electric cars and demonstrate their usage.

There is no mention here of barbed-wire fences, but Mr. Currier indicates that he has marked as an exhibit for the hearing the front and back covers of a book Ned sent him—*Solo: Life with an Electric Car,* by Noel Perrin:

> The front and back covers specifically note your literary status and interest in electric cars and the prologue notes both your academic position, as well as your intent and action on integrating the issue of electric cars in the classroom.

Mr. Currier's prose style is a little bewildering, but I forgive him because he is such a good sport. He says at the end,

> If you do not feel that this information, as discussed, is sufficient evidence of the importance of your driver's license, you may instruct the Hearing Examiner at the time of your hearing of any other pertinent parts of the book you wish entered into the record.

This seems very decent of him.

Currier's next letter to Ned, of April 28, with attached findings by hearing examiner Melinda H. Tobin, is discouraging. The findings are very clear, and for anyone who loved Ned, they are painful to read. Ms. Tobin includes this information:

> Under 23 U.S.A. Statute 636, the Petitioner's suspension must remain in effect until such time as he undertakes and passes a written examination, as part of an annually required examination due to the Petitioner's degenerative neurological condition.

Ms. Tobin outlines again Ned's argument that he needs to continue driving an electric car in order to teach his Environmental Studies class. She also reveals a second argument of Ned's, a new one to me:

. . . he has historically been in the position of administering multiple choice examinations and has not been in the position of taking them. Therefore, he asserts that he should be exempt from re-taking the multiple choice, written examination because he holds a "strong internal resistance" to doing so.

What? Ned has a "strong internal resistance" to *taking* multiple-choice examinations because he has been accustomed only to *giving* multiple-choice examinations?

Go, Professor Perrin!

All the same, Ms. Tobin's eleven-page document tactfully and compassionately informs Professor Perrin that her hands are tied by the laws of the state of Vermont:

. . . it appears the Petitioner has developed an emotional response toward re-taking the examination. Considering the Petitioner's intellectual and professional accomplishments, such an emotional response is not only reasonable, it might even be expected. It does not, however, preclude him from the examination requirement.

In her conclusion, the hearing examiner writes,

that the indefinite suspension issued to the Petitioner, Noel Perrin, for failure to pass a written examination is appropriate and proper.

The next document in the yellow folder is—you guessed it—a SUSPENSION/REVOCATION/DISQUALIFICATION notice, dated May 5, 2003. This is the fourth one.

You'd think that would be the end of the story, wouldn't you? I would, too, and we'd both be wrong. On May 22, 2003, Ned wrote another letter, this one directly to Hearing Examiner Tobin, on his Dartmouth Environmental Studies Program letterhead. This is the first part of it:

Dear Melinda Tobin,

I think I am overcoming my neurosis about the written test that is part of getting one's driver's license reinstated.

He does not explain his speedy recovery from neurosis, but he asks a few questions about retaking the test, and expresses his appreciation for the hearing examiner's "very kind phone call, back in April."

There is a response dated May 28. It comes not from the compassionate Ms. Tobin but from the very efficient Gordon P. Currier, the AOT Policy and Hearings chief, reminding Ned that he must apply to the DMV, not the Hearings Unit, "for any further information that you require regarding driving examinations."

Mysteriously, there are four copies of Mr. Currier's May 28 letter to Ned in the file, but there is only one more letter written by Ned himself. It is dated "17 June, 2003" and it is addressed to the commissioner of motor vehicles. It is typed, once again, on Dartmouth College Environmental Studies Program letterhead, and it fills the page. I noticed as I read the letter that a few typographical and spelling errors are present, for the first time in this correspondence. Suggestion is "suggedtion," "of" is typed "pg," and Mr. Currier's name is "Cuerier" in one instance:

Dear Commissioner Rutledge,

I am writing to you at the suggestion of Mr. Gordon Currier, and I am writing to ask your help. Help with what? With regaining the right to operate a car . . .

The arguments presented before are presented again: Ned needs his driver's license to continue teaching an environmental studies course at Dartmouth, with special emphasis on electric cars. He has failed the multiple-choice written driver's examination, and he has a "strong neurotic aversion" to taking it again (a relapse, evidently, since his letter to Ms. Tobin in May).

If it is absolutely imperative that he take the exam again, he asks Commissioner Rutledge that he be permitted to take it in Montpelier, rather than Springfield, which is far from his Thetford home. He encloses a copy of *Solo: Life with an Electric Car,* and he says he does not want it back. He suggests, "Possibly someone at the DMV would enjoy reading it." I am sure someone would, because it's a wonderful book.

Always fair-minded, Ned admits to the commissioner at the end of his letter that he might have misrepresented Gordon P. Currier's interest in his cause:

> When I said that Mr. Currier suggested that I write the DMV, I did not mean that he supports my request. I take him to be at best neutral.

The next paragraph is a sentence of only six words:

> And now it is time to stop.

Apparently, he did. Tucked in among the accident and insurance forms at the back of the folder is a letter to Sara, dated February 3, 2004, from Amica Mutual Insurance Company, with her husband's name at the top as "Driver: Noel Perrin." The letter states simply, "We are removing the above driver from the list of operators in your household."

When I closed the folder quickly after reading this letter, I saw that on its yellow cover there was something written in pencil. It was in Ned's handwriting, though it was hard to read because some of the letters were much tinier than others, even within a single word. The words were "Com. Of DMV Bonnie Rutledge."

I have a message for you, Bonnie Rutledge, and for Melinda Tobin, and Gordon P. Currier, and all the good people at the DMV. I know you could not give Noel Perrin his license back. In fact, many years before he had Parkinson's, I sometimes wondered how Ned ever got a driver's license in the first place. But don't you miss him anyway, just a little? I know now, because of you, how very, very much I miss him, too. Thank you.

12. The End-of-the-Road Writers

Once a month, usually on Monday and more or less at noon, a group of writers meets at my house, at the end of our dirt road in northern Vermont. Some of us refer to ourselves as the "End-of-the-Road Writers Group." I can't speak for the other writers, but this label feels appropriate to me in many of my writing moods, and sometimes I feel even more like an "End of Her Rope at the End of the Road" writer: blocked, frustrated, and lonely. That's why it's so nice to have company.

There can be as many as ten of us or as few as three at any given meeting. Some writers have published their work, some hope to do so, a few aren't sure or aren't telling. They bring ongoing works of fiction, nonfiction, and poetry to share, either by reading the work aloud to the assembled group or passing around copies of a manuscript before the meeting. We have diverse backgrounds and divergent interests: organic farming, fly-fishing, memoir, religion, biography.

Along with our writing, we share food. One writer brings deviled eggs because the rest of us would be so disappointed if he didn't. He makes delicious deviled eggs, and he has been documenting a search for someone close to him in childhood who disappeared from his life almost sixty years ago. Now that he has found her, he is writing about what that experience has been like for both of them.

Another writer brings homemade soup cooked with vegetables from her garden. She writes about the clashing overt and subterranean agendas within the organic movement in American agriculture, from its early history to the present day.

I am writing this book, along with a couple of books for very young children. I bake an egg-and-cheese concoction made from a recipe given me by another writer, my old friend Ellie Newton.

"Aunt Ellie's Cheese Puff" is a little like a soufflé, only it is much easier to make, and doesn't ever fall in on itself in the oven the way soufflés do, collapsing like swooning swans in ballet performances. Aunt Ellie lived to be 104 with all her faculties intact and her heart pumping nicely, so I'm not as concerned about cholesterol as I probably should be with this dish. Still, I use "low-carb" bread if I can find some in the store, on behalf of my friends on the Atkins diet.

Ellie shared her poems and her recipes as generously as she shared herself, so I will include this in her memory:

AUNT ELLIE'S CHEESE PUFF (SERVES 8–10)

For Full Recipe:

3 to 5 eggs

2½ cups milk

4 cups buttered and diced bread

4 cups cheese (cheddar or other strong cheese)

dry mustard

salt and pepper to taste*

*I use Vermont cheddar cheese, and omit the salt

Preheat oven to 400° F.

Mix eggs and milk in bowl, stir briskly, set aside. (A good ratio is 1 egg to ½ cup milk, but can be altered to taste.)

Place in a buttered 9" x 13" casserole: one layer bread cubes, one layer cheese, sprinkling each layer with mustard, salt, and pepper. Repeat until dish is well filled, finishing with layer of cheese.

Pour egg-milk mixture over all, then bake for 45 minutes to 1 hour.

I often cut the recipe in half (2 cups bread, 2 cups cheese, 2 to 3 eggs, $1\frac{1}{4}$ cup milk), bake it in a pie pan, and serve it to a small group. You don't have to be a writer to enjoy this but unless they are more tactful than truthful, my writer friends like it a lot.

People bring chicken salad and tuna salad and hummus and vegetable dips and crackers and desserts. There is always plenty of food, and there are always plenty of people for good conversation. Still, each month on the morning the writers group meets, I worry about two things:

1) Will anybody show up?
2) Will there be enough to eat?

These two concerns are inherently contradictory, I know. If nobody comes to the meeting, as per worry #1, then nobody needs to eat, making worry #2 irrelevant. All the same, on writers-group days I rush to the market early just in case, picking up cranberry juice and cider and bread and sandwich meats, things my family will happily consume if the writers don't.

For an early spring writers-group meeting this year I bought fruit, thinking I'd make a fruit salad to cheer us all up during a dreary season. I got bananas and apples and grapes, a cantaloupe, and a couple of kiwis. Then I got an avocado and a tomato, too, telling myself that I might decide to make a green salad instead. I really bought the tomato because on that cold, drizzly day in the middle of March, it was so enticingly red and round, a bright plump sphere in a dark and shapeless world.

I noticed when I unpacked the grocery bags that the tomato had come from Mexico, along with its friend the avocado. This turned out to be a very cosmopolitan collection I had brought home from the White Market in St. Johnsbury in mid-March. The kiwi was Italian, the strawberries had flown in from Chile, and the bananas came from Guatemala, bearing a picture of the lady who wears the big hat with all the fruit on it. I have admired her since childhood. Anybody who can wear a hat like that deserves respect.

As I sliced up the fruit in my kitchen I imagined the writers were bumping along the back roads to get here (if anybody was coming). They weren't flying in from Central America, they were driving along Joe's Brook Road in Barnet, or up over Crow Hill in St. Johnsbury. These roads are icy in February and muddy in April, and in March they were something unpleasantly in between. I could not quite believe that my friends really wanted to travel on them, and all the way down our own icy, muddy road to the end.

It's a casual group. Attendance is always optional, but I knew some of the writers were planning to be here because I'd spoken with them since our last meeting. Still, they might forget, or their cars might break down, or they might wake up in one of those moods writers have, when you just can't stand to share your work with another writer or to risk hurting someone's feelings by making an honest comment about work they have shared with you.

Food is so much easier. If you like somebody's food, you eat it and you go back for seconds. If you have reservations you try a very small portion, and if you don't like what you're eating you can always mess the food around on the plate with your fork, so it looks as if you had consumed more than you did.

You don't ever have to tell a friend that you think the dish should have been prepared with more salt or less pepper. You are not called upon to say that it seems a bit bland or a touch overdramatic. With food you don't have to be a critic, you just chew and swallow, with your mouth shut.

Sharing writing is very different. The trouble with belonging to a group like ours is that you bring to it your food, your work, and your sensitive self, and the others in the group naturally respond to all three. That's what the group is for. Nobody criticizes the food, partly for the reasons outlined above, and also because we meet at noon and we're hungry. Furthermore, we are well-behaved, courteous adults. Nobody would dream of saying, "I hate hummus!" or, "You're giving us that cheese-egg-and-bread glop *again?*"

None among us would consciously disparage another person's writing, either, but writers tend to be touchy and sensitive to criticism, just like other people and maybe a little more so. I confess that on my part, any positive comment about my written work can inspire giddy exhilaration, while a mild negative remark may cause me to mumble and pace the floor, figuratively speaking, for hours.

In my heart of hearts I don't even like to have my typographical errors pointed out. When this happens I sweetly thank the person who discovered the mistake, and I say something like, "Oh, for heaven's sake! I've been over this ten times and I never noticed—how could I have missed that?" Internally, I'm pouting, pacing, and mumbling, *Okay, so maybe "this" is not spelled "thix," but it should be.*

This is ridiculous, and I apologize, but I think that having your writing criticized is a little like having someone point out a flaw or a malfeasance in your child. Regardless of the offense, some instinct leaps up in protest.

What do you mean, "obscene graffiti"? Look at that beautiful penmanship!

In a writers group, commentary and criticism are what we are here for, beyond the companionship and the deviled eggs, even beyond the imported avocados. These, someone once warned me, may be loaded to their pretty pits with pesticides that farmers are not allowed to use in this country but are permitted to use in others. I washed my avocado very well, knowing I was about to feed it to my friends, and I thought about invisible toxins, and about writers in groups.

The combination of diversity and sensitivity within a writers group is really its greatest asset but only if one can survive the richness of the mix. So many different opinions spread around a room can be dangerous if people are not skillful in what they say and how they say it.

Critical commentary is a lot like chicken manure. Properly applied, chicken manure is a great fertilizer, and well-aged chicken manure is "pure gold," a gardening friend told me. But misunderstood or misused, too raw or too strong, the stuff not only smells terrible but will burn and destroy a whole garden.

I can still recall one horrible moment during a writing seminar back in college, when a sneering student said of a classmate's novel, "It reads like something you'd pick up in an airport." He did not mean this as a compliment, even though most writers then and now would be delighted to have their books "picked up in an airport," or anywhere else for that matter.

I remember how glad I was that the professor immediately chastised the speaker for his discourtesy, and how relieved I was that the remark had been made about someone else, not me. At that age, just hearing such a nasty tone of voice directed toward my work might have prevented me from ever writing another word. Fortunately the novelist was a man of middle age and easy temperament. He appeared, at least, to be unperturbed.

Aside from being appallingly rude, the student was confusing personal taste with an objective response to a manuscript *on its own terms.* He may not have been interested in "airport" fiction, any more than I was impressed by his own endless unpunctuated sentences and obvious borrowings from Proust, Joyce, and Faulkner. That was not the point. In a writing seminar, as in a writers group, people come together from vast literary distances, as far removed from one another as the Italian kiwis and the Chilean strawberries. These people might never meet and surely would not read each other's work in any other context.

No writer has to like another's writing. I'm convinced that some writers never do like anybody else's writing. They are interested only in their own work. But what the writers in a group do have to do, and what I knew those in our group would do at my house that day (if anybody came, and if everybody had enough to eat), is find out what other writers need in the way of support, and then try to provide that support. That's all there is to it.

It sounds easy, but it isn't. One difficulty is that too often people coming to a writers group will say, "Please tell me what you think about this piece I have written, and be sure to tell me the truth, whatever it is." The atmosphere created by such an open-ended statement is a kind of literary/emotional minefield, for both reader and writer. No two readers respond the same way to any piece of writing, and the fledgling writer who hears everything that everybody thinks about a piece, "whatever it is," may sink into a dismal swamp of conflicting opinions, and drown.

One writer in our group, who has since left us partly for this reason, was told by a group member that an essay seemed "too subjective and personal." Another member of the group thought the tone of the same piece was "distanced and aloof." The writer was confused and upset, felt attacked on two sides, and quit.

A writer sharing work this way should be very clear about what kind of response he or she is looking for. People need to know, for instance, if someone can't stand to have their writing dissected technically, sliced up for examination line by line like a Guatemalan banana ("On page five, paragraph two, I noticed a split infinitive"). Otherwise the writer will be hurt and the readers will be baffled. *I don't get it—what did she want me to do?*

You may want your spelling mistakes corrected and your typographical errors pointed out. I don't, but you might. If not, there is nothing wrong with telling the group, "This is probably full of spelling errors and typos, but I can take care of those later. What I want to know now is whether I should write more about specific legislation . . ."; or, "I'd like to know whether the character of the mother is well defined . . .; or, "I want to know if it's funny . . ."

It is hard for some writers to hear so many differing comments about their work, no matter how specific these may be. I have found that getting conflicting responses can be helpful, though. Someone commented recently that a chapter I was working on seemed overburdened with dates. They might provide accuracy, he said, but including so many of them bogged down the narrative. I listened to him, agreed, and trimmed back the dates. Then I shared the piece with the group again. A different writer sent me back my manuscript with this notation in one margin: "Include date here! The reader needs it."

I smiled at the contradiction, but on reflection I think both critics were right. First I had too many dates in the piece, making it read like a bus schedule. Then I cut back too drastically and lost the sense of events and experiences occurring within a real time period. With help, I found the right balance.

When I get a piece of writing back with appreciative comments in the margins, I am thrilled. When I am reading aloud, I love to hear somebody laugh at my jokes, or to see out of the corner of my eye that someone is nodding agreement with some insight. After I have finished reading, it means a great deal to me if somebody says, "I loved what you wrote about mothers and daughters," or, best of all, "I can't wait to hear more!" I want to run right back to my desk and write.

It takes courage to share a piece of writing, especially in its early stages when the writer is not sure about what has been written so far, and doesn't know where to go next. But writers are brave. They have to be. They need courage to keep on writing in spite of isolation and rejection, in spite of clumsy—or even skillful—criticism, and over the objections of private demons and up against the barriers of internal obstacles. They just keep on writing. They go on. Through the mud and the icy patches, over the back roads in bad weather, they keep on going, and once a month some of them arrive at my house, here at the end of the road.

As I finished slicing up the fruit I saw somebody coming up the steps with a covered dish in his hands. Deviled eggs! There was another car pulling up by the barn, and a third one not far behind. I put the sliced fruit in the bowl, wiped my hands on a dishtowel, and went to open the door.

13. Winter Reading,
Summer Reading

I love to read. I read not just for education and entertainment but also, I think, as a way of maintaining consistency in the life of my mind. I have felt this way ever since I first learned how to read silently, when I was about six. I thought it was magical, miraculous. Finally I could leave behind the slow, out-loud, word-by-word deciphering of my 1950s reading textbooks and their tediously repetitive stories about Alice and Jerry and Dick and Jane and Baby Sally. Even at that young age I knew that these people were not very interesting. It seemed to me they were not very intelligent, either. They had to keep reminding each other to watch the dog.

"See Spot. See Sally. See Dick. See Jane. See Spot. See Spot run. Run, Spot, run!"

Poor Spot was probably running away from this family of morons, I thought as I diligently read the stories out loud nonetheless, following word by boring word with my pointing finger moving across the page, intoning one tedious sentence after another. Finally, my family couldn't stand it any longer. My sister showed me how to read silently.

It happened during a family trip to Florida in a trailer my parents owned at that time. We were parked near the Everglades, and it felt just as hot and steamy inside the trailer as it did outside. I remember the interior as very like the cabin in a boat: compact, with small spaces and shiny wood surfaces. I sat on a bench at a table, both attached to the trailer's side wall, while my sister, Anne, determinedly showed me that I could read with my mouth shut. I knew that if I valued my health, I'd better.

My sister gave me some better books as a reward, and before long I was reading the C. S. Lewis Narnia series. I never looked back.

From that time on I have been reading nonstop in every location and climate, all year round. It is only since living in northern Vermont that I've sometimes elected to choose my reading matter seasonally. In very cold weather, I gravitate toward hot stuff, in a literary sense. For all of one really unforgiving February I was reading Isak Dinesen's *Out of Africa* upstairs at bedtime to counteract the frost on the windowpanes and the howling winds, and I kept Gabriel García Márquez's *One Hundred Years of Solitude* downstairs so I could huddle by the fireplace in the living room and read at odd moments during the day.

I had read *Out of Africa* before and have read it again since that winter—Isak Dinesen is a favorite writer, whose books my mother introduced me to many years ago. But I was reading *One Hundred Years of Solitude* for the first time. I was only reading it out of cold weather desperation; I didn't think I was going to like it, having picked up the book ten years back and scanned the first line, "Years later, as he faced the firing squad . . . ," before putting it down again.

Any book whose first sentence contained a firing squad was not for me, I figured, no matter how wildly my friends raved about it. I'm the kind of person whose children routinely say, "You should close your eyes here, Mom," when we watch movies on television together. If anything bad is going to happen to a human being or an animal, I don't want to witness it, or read about it. However, this one February was really, really cold, so I relented.

I'm so thankful I did. To this day I don't feel sure whether I read *One Hundred Years of Solitude* or dreamed it, maybe during a long Vermont hibernation. It was the geography and climate that appealed to me when I began to read. The enchantment came later. When I started reading the book, I only knew that I was willing to put up with firing squads and magic realism in Márquez, as I had been willing to spend time with displaced aristocratic Danes in Isak Dinesen's East Africa, as long as it made me feel warm.

Another appealing thing about both of these books was that they were written long ago. I like a well-aged book. Like a vintage wine or a thoughtfully aging woman—ahem!—an old book has substance and character and a lot of words I have to look up. This is an exercise I enjoy, odd as that may seem. I like old words, like "fulsome" and "troglodyte," and collect them when I get the chance. If I find one that isn't too hard to read and spell, I'll put it in a children's book. Children appreciate good words, too.

I don't have anything against contemporary writers. Aside from cold weather idiosyncrasies, I like to read books from all eras at all times, often in fairly large doses. Last year I read one Philip Roth, though not the one in which my father appears, as well as two Tracy Chevaliers and a new Chris Bohjalian, all between Thanksgiving and Christmas. Sometimes I read several examples of a certain kind of book, say mystery or memoir, or many books by one author, be it D. H. Lawrence or Sara Paretsky. When I'm starting a book-binge, I never know where it will take me.

When I read Dan Brown's religious/mystery books *(The Da Vinci Code, Angels & Demons)* I traveled down a new path, and it took me to an older one. The most interesting thing to me about these books was the way the author wove together the vicissitudes of human nature and the foibles of organized religion. While reading, I thought of another author whose work I had not read for years: Anthony Trollope.

It was my sister, Anne, again, who first introduced me to Trollope. She handed me a copy of *Barchester Towers* about twenty years ago, and this was the book I thought of after finishing the Dan Brown mysteries. I went searching for *Barchester Towers* all over the house, and finally found it on the bookshelf next to my bed: a worn, leather-bound New Century Library edition published by Thomas Nelson and Sons, Ltd. (London, Edinburgh, and New York). I was happy at first, then frustrated.

The book I held in my hand was printed long enough ago that the "New Century" referred to was the twentieth. It measures $4\frac{1}{4}$ by $6\frac{1}{4}$ inches, and between its covers are 583 tiny, near-transparent pages, each of them covered with astonishingly small print. I must have had bigger eyes and smaller fingers the last time I read this book.

Fortunately, I was able to borrow a readable copy of *Barchester Towers* and several other books by Trollope from a friend. She had newer and larger editions with fonts of reasonable size. Better yet, they were paperbacks, published within recent memory by Oxford University Press, Wordsworth Classics, and Dover Publications. I was very grateful to her.

I borrowed the books in the summer of 2004, in anticipation of my first trip to Europe in about fifteen years. Anthony Trollope became a very important element in that journey. I would be traveling to Europe by plane, and the plan was that I'd be in the company of a beloved cousin who was going to visit a college friend in southern France, and my son, Ben, then sixteen, who had been accepted at a six-week summer film program in Paris.

When we got to the airport in Boston, we found that Ben had left his passport at home in Vermont. After a lot of fast-talking and long-distance phone calls from Logan Airport, my cousin's husband and daughter housed Ben overnight and made arrangements to get the passport and to put him on the same plane the next day. Meanwhile, because the airline needed three seats together and we no longer would be using all of them, my cousin and I were upgraded to business class. Everybody was happy.

My plans for the European trip involved seeing friends and relatives in several countries, so I intended to travel lightly and efficiently: the emotional burden of nostalgia mixed with apprehension was heavy enough. I had my passport and I had a bank card, but no traveler's checks for the first time in all my travels to Europe over the years. I had learned from a daughter working at a bed-and-breakfast in France that I really didn't need them. I had my travel schedule arranged. I had my hotel reservations in order. I just couldn't make up my mind about the most important thing of all.

What was I going to read?

I had no idea how I would be feeling from day to day, or even from minute to minute. I wanted to read something that would offer me calm and a kind of grounding, along with something to laugh about. What a joy it was, after boarding a train in Paris or Berlin, after lifting, rolling, and haplessly hauling my suitcase down the aisles and finding my compartment and my seat, after finally sitting down and settling in to enjoy the trip and think about what might be at the end of each section of it, what a delight to open a book whose first sentence sedately and deliciously read:

> There are women who cannot grow alone as standard trees;—for whom the support and warmth of some wall, some paling, some post, is absolutely necessary . . . *(Rachel Ray)*

or:

I am disposed to believe that no novel reader in England has seen the little town of Bullhampton, in Wiltshire, except such novel readers as live there . . . *(The Vicar of Bullhampton)*

or:

Sir Harry Hotspur of Humblethwaite was a mighty person in Cumberland . . . *(Sir Harry Hotspur of Humblethwaite)*

This was exactly what I needed: quiet words in measured tones and in a rhythm that would steady any pulse. It was like listening to Bach, only funnier.

Until I revisited *Barchester Towers,* I'd forgotten all about that exquisitely slimy pillar of the episcopacy, Obadiah Slope. I'd also let slip from my memory the lovely Madeline Vesey Neroni, a beautiful woman whose injuries have made her frail and whose claim to royal Italian connections is dubious. She makes up for all this with a wonderfully lavish vanity. The Signora Neroni always sends a servant to visit her hosts, for instance, before any gala occasion. She has to know whether the sofa to which her delicate person will be transported is a "right or a left hand sofa," so that she may arrange her jewels, ribbons, and her magnificent self accordingly.

As a writer of novels about his own era, Trollope could be a keen and strident critic not only of his contemporaries but also of his literary colleagues. He was not an admirer of Dickens, whom he caricatures as "Mr. Sentiment" in thinly disguised references, and neither the government, nor any political party, nor the upper classes, nor the church escape his relentless scrutiny. All in all, for nuances of character and custom, for a steady, even unrolling of narration and plot, and for the occasional merciless skewering of pretension, there is nobody like Trollope. He was the perfect choice for the European trip. I'm so glad I had him with me that summer. It also occurred to me that if anybody asked what I did with myself that summer, and I didn't want to say too much about it, I could always tell the truth by saying, "I traveled all through Europe with three Trollopes on the train."

14. Birds Again

It is the month of May. The grass is growing, the apple blossoms are blossoming, and we are being bullied by the birds again.

It happens every year. First the bluebirds come, in early April. They harass my husband as he walks up the hill behind the farmhouse to check on the sheep fence in preparation for letting the flock out to graze. The male bluebird flies from fence post to fence post, complaining nonstop:

> *Where's my house? Why isn't my house ready yet? What have you been doing all winter?*

Nat puts up bluebird houses all over the farm: on the fence posts along the side of the pasture, in the orchard, and in the fields. He cleans these beautiful little pitched-roofed wooden boxes every spring, clearing out the nesting materials and other debris from last year to make their homes ready for this season's new families. The bluebirds have no patience with him until the boxes are ready. Then they can move in and begin making more bluebirds, who will bully him next year at the same time. Nat won't say so because he loves them, but his bluebirds are ungrateful, self-centered, and rude.

Next, the cliff swallows arrive. Without so much as a knock on our door, they start building their mud-daubed nests all over our house, under the eaves on both sides of the building and in the corners of the porch roof. The nests are shaped like upside-down igloos, with a round hole in each one through which the birds can fly in and out, and from which they can spy on us and yell at us.

At least three nests go up along the underside of the main roof by the front door, the door we don't use at all in winter because it's blocked off to keep the heat from escaping and the cold from coming in. Two more nests are constructed in the under-corners of the porch roof, just opposite the door we use to go in and out of the house every day all year.

Whichever door we use, the nesting swallows don't like it. They swoop in and out over our heads, they chitter and scold from their corners, they argue with the dog and they chatter with each other. No matter how discreetly we try to get into or out of our home—not letting the door slam, not talking too loudly as we go by—the swallows have something to say about it.

They don't miss a thing. When I get up in the morning and let the dog out, a small head with a yellow beak pokes out immediately from the little mud-nest hole high up to my left, and another one emerges from its fellow on the right. They like to check on our every movement, then they make comments, like gossipy neighbors:

> *The boy will be late for school again, I bet! You are*
> *so right. That woman could sleep through the Second*
> *Coming!*

We have what I think of as a "working porch." On it there are farm necessities as well as boxes of books and other materials coming in and going out with delivery trucks that speed into the dooryard regularly. There are cross-country skis and ski poles leaning against the wall in winter, and garden tools and flowerpots in baskets and on benches in summer. The mop stands out on the porch to dry, and hanging on a wooden peg is a lead rope attached to a halter no longer in use but impossible to give away. It belonged to my last, best Morgan horse, Dulcie, who died three days after her thirtieth birthday a couple of years ago.

There is a bristly boot scraper by the door, one of those things that are supposed to help keep the dirt outdoors, though that isn't really why we have it. It feels like a hedgehog and it is shaped like a turtle. Because I am fond of both hedgehogs and turtles I bought it as soon as I saw it at the Vermont Country Store, and I put it on the porch because that's were it belongs. Once in a while somebody even uses it to scrape their boots.

But best of all, there are two really comfortable rocking chairs on the porch, with a small wooden table between them. Nat and I love to sit in these chairs on summer evenings and watch the sun go down. We swat black flies together, we talk about our children and the government, and we can see our fields in the near view and beyond them the wooded hills and the darkening sky.

We can't do that now, and we won't be able to do it for many weeks to come, because the swallows are nesting. We don't want to disturb them. We don't even turn on the porch light at night during this period. Our guests and our visiting children stumble up and down the steps in the dark while the swallows sit and snicker from their cozy corners high above:

Did you see that? I thought for sure he'd end up in the rose-bush. Me, too. Oh, well, there's always tomorrow night . . .

They don't hesitate to disturb *us*, of course. If we venture even briefly onto the porch in search of a shovel or a mop, the birds nag at us incessantly in their squeaky voices. They make a sound like a dozen small doors with creaking hinges, opening and shutting and opening and shutting and opening and shutting, with nobody going anywhere. It's enough to drive you crazy.

And there are others. A robin scolded me viciously—a robin!—when I started up the road to take a walk, just because her bumbling, just-fledged baby was flapping less than gracefully from the shed roof on one side of the dirt road to a low branch of the apple tree on the other side. A hummingbird hovered and buzzed at my husband's knees when Nat inadvertently came too close for hummingbird comfort. The barn swallows, fork-tailed avengers from another branch of the swallow family, will dive-bomb anybody who goes into the barn at the wrong time to feed the chickens.

Chickens? The chickens are the worst of all. For one thing, we always have too many roosters. Somehow every brood of darling baby chicks contains twice as many strutting, crowing, hen-chasing cockerels as it does demure egg-producing pullets. Not content to practice their hoarse and half-strangled adolescent cock-a-doodle-doos all day long, the little roosters chase the little hens all around the yard, sometimes three or four young men after one young lady, the hen squawking at a high pitch and run-ning just as fast as she can, feathers lifted like the skirts of some poultry princess fleeing from the ball.

I'm never absolutely sure whether the hen is really trying to escape or whether she's just being coy, but I don't want to think about it.

This kind of activity in the barnyard inspired a gift to my writer husband from his oldest son: a handsome, very lifelike model of a bantam rooster with a gaudy arc of tail feathers and a prurient plastic eye. It is mounted on a polished wood back-ground, with a brass plaque that reads, "Pullet Surprise: Nat

Tripp, 2003." We love it. We may have been living and writing in Vermont for too many years.

With all of this going on, there are bound to be many more baby chicks, including many more roosters. Thus the cycle continues. During the time when the hens are setting, moreover, and for a while after their chicks have hatched, the hens can be scary, too. I went out to the barn last week to visit a mother and her new baby chicks. I had discovered them that morning, seven fuzzy chicks with the charmingly striped, black-and-brown coloring of chipmunks, only they were even smaller than chipmunks, because these are bantams. When I opened the door to the empty sheep stall where I had first seen the mother and her new brood, the hen flew up in the air with her claws out to attack me, in ruffled fury. I was just leaving food and water, for heaven's sake!

Hens are fiercely protective of their offspring at this time of year, but they have flawed and limited maternal instincts, in my opinion. Or maybe they just can't count.

"Seven chicks?" Nat looked up when I reported my find. "That hen had her nest up in the hayloft. I saw her with her chicks yesterday, I forgot to tell you. But there were ten of them."

I decided to look in the hayloft for the missing chicks. I went out to the barn again and climbed up the ladder to the loft, where we store six hundred or more bales of hay for the sheep each year. We make hay when (if!) the sun shines, with the help of our children and friends.

I say "we," because I have a minor role in the operation, but it is Nat who does most of the work, using ancient and marginally functional farm machinery from another age. With tractor and cutter bar he mows the hayfields a little at a time, hoping not to have any of it rained upon. He lets the hay dry for a couple of days, "tedding" it to fluff it up and help the process along, then rakes it into long ribbons of windrows. From these he eventually makes the bales with a venerable, cantankerous baler that must be almost as old as we are.

The kids and I help him load the bales into the back of the pickup truck, fifty-four bales to a load that is exactly five bales high and arranged exactly the same way each time, according to a system Nat has developed to allow for the wheel wells in the truck bed and to assure the stability of the load as it builds.

When the pickup is full Nat drives to the barn, sometimes with the kids riding on the top of the whole fragrant, swaying mass, always with barn swallows swooping and protesting overhead. Then each person takes a position up in the loft while Nat turns the switch for the hay elevator and begins to haul the bales off the back of the truck. He sends them clanking up on the elevator, one by one, to be stacked again by the crew above him in piles on the loft floor, not very far from where I found the tiny dead bodies of three fuzzy black-and-brown chicks last week, right at the top of my ladder. Eight, nine, and ten, from the bantam hen's new brood.

"They didn't dare jump," said Nat when I told him. "We can't get too upset about it."

But I always do. Even after thirty-odd years of country living, with all the dead chicks, dead lambs, dead dogs, and dead horses, the hamsters, the rabbits, the lizards, and the turtles (not to mention, dear God, the people!), I still get upset about it.

I know it isn't really the hen's fault. She lays her eggs in the hayloft for protection, and when her chicks hatch up there she expects them to jump down to the barn floor, eight feet below, so they can begin to live their chicken lives. If some of them can't or won't follow their mother and die for their reluctance, so be it. The hen can't go back and persuade the stragglers to take the plunge, as it were. She has to care for the others. It is a hen's nature.

It is my nature to hate having these things happen, though, and I do. So does Nat, no matter what he says. He has admitted that he's watched this hen in other years, and has worried enough about the great leap she and each of her successive families must take from the hayloft that he has sometimes placed bales at regular intervals along the hay elevator, which leans against the loft floor at its top and has its base on the ground. He hopes the mother hen will understand what he has done and will use these bales as steps to make the downward journey easier for her family. I don't know whether she has ever taken the hint. Do hens take hints?

A week after I first saw them, I am pleased to see that this hen still has all seven of her remaining chicks. They follow closely behind her through the barnyard and across the dirt driveway to our lawn every day, peeping and cheeping and bouncing along like so many fuzzy Ping-Pong balls. I'm so pleased about this that I almost forget the chickens are headed for my perennial beds, but not quite. When I shoo them back to the barnyard, they all bounce and peep again. Their peeping, like the squeaking of the nesting swallows, is a unique sound, one I have often tried to duplicate but have always failed to get quite right.

Birds are hard to imitate. Perhaps for this reason, I've never had much luck communicating with them, with one exception.

We had a finch living in our house for four years. This bird was given to us by my younger daughter at the time she was moving to California. It was a zebra finch, a female, and she lived in a cage. She had come from a pet store in New York City, but her ancestors surely must have flitted and chirped in the tropical forests of a warmer hemisphere. Like me many years before her, she was a newcomer to northern Vermont.

This bird was very small, and she was all alone in her cage, a pretty, solitary prisoner. I hung the cage in the living room where people would come by often because I felt so sorry for her. I always feel sorry for caged and penned-in creatures, hypocritical as that may seem coming from a sheep owner and the mother of children who have grown up with so many small exotic pets from other parts of the world, hamsters and hedgehogs and all.

My sympathy was a bit tempered when my daughter told me before she left for the coast that this bird's name was Murder Bird. Every other bird she had tried to keep in the cage with it, including its original mate from the pet store, ended up dead.

But she was a nice bird to live with, homicidal tendencies notwithstanding. She fluttered and chirped happily when I played the piano, even if it was, as it often was, a very awkward and mistake-riddled rendition of the first Prelude from Bach's *Well-Tempered Clavier*, played over and over again. Every time I passed the cage on the way to the washing machine in the back hall to do the laundry she would chirp at me, too. It was a pleasant, midrange chirp, a little less juicy and drawn-out than the chirping of the robin on the lawn in spring, but just as cheerful a sound.

It was a very tempting noise, in fact, and before long I began to chirp right back. I couldn't help it. The finch got really excited about this. She hopped up and down in her perch and let loose a long string of energetic birdsong, which I then imitated, to which she immediately responded, and so forth.

We went on this way for four years until about a month ago when the finch gently died. She fluttered to the floor of the cage, sat quietly there for a day or two declining to eat or drink, and that was it. I assume she died of natural causes rather than from the strain of being insulted, or assaulted by gibberish, every time I went by her cage. Who knows what I said, after all? Not me.

I miss the little finch, but to be perfectly honest I don't miss her much. That is, I miss her quite a bit more than the three baby chicks, and a lot more than any of the hamsters we've housed— I've never been able to feel warm and cuddly about rodents—but I miss her a thousand times less than any dog I've ever owned in my life, including the awful ones.

She was good company in her way, but we didn't have that kind of relationship. We kept to ourselves, except for the chirping. That's where I'm having trouble.

It is just so hard for me not to chirp.

For four years, I chirped three or four times a day or even more. I chirped every single time I walked through the living room, and I got an answering chirp in return. I liked this, and I miss it. For both of us it was a kind of acknowledgment.

Hello, I'm still here, are you? Hello, and yes, I'm here, too.

Not just one voice has gone from that conversation, but two, and I miss the sound of mine as much as I miss the other. With all the squeaking and squawking and peeping and chittering outdoors at this time of year, under the eaves and in the barn, on the lawn and in the fields and in the woods, it seems unfair that when I pass by the one place where I could add my own voice to the chorus of birdsong, I now have to bite my lip.

But sometimes when there are no other people in the house, I chirp anyway, just as much as I want to, and just as loud as I can. Why not? Only a few feet from where I'm standing, on the other side of the wall, everybody else is doing it, too.

15. Drugs

When I pulled a muscle in my back the other day, I went to the
medicine cabinet immediately, found a bottle of ibuprofen, and
took three pills (600 mg) for the pain. My ninety-year-old mother-
in-law had a heart attack a couple of years ago and is still arguing
with her doctor about taking medication of any kind. She says that
every prescription she ever filled made her feel worse than the
complaint for which it was prescribed. If something really hurts,
she might be persuaded to take half a baby aspirin. Our pharmacist
tells me this would give her about 40 mg of medication, a negligi-
ble dose. My mother-in-law and I are thirty years apart in age. She
distrusts drugs, I rely on them. Is it a generational thing?

I certainly hope so. As I and the other members of this much-
publicized "Sixties Generation" go through our own sixties—and
seventies and eighties and (we secretly hope) beyond—the least
we can do for ourselves is live up to our own mythology, and take
lots of drugs.

I am thinking of legal drugs, this time. I was not much involved
with the other kind even in my youth, though there was that one
time in 1965 when I ate a piece of hashish fudge made from a recipe
in *The Alice B. Toklas Cookbook*. I cannot recall today whether the
cookbook was compiled by Miss Toklas herself or whether it was

the work of her friend and companion Gertrude Stein, whose writing I have always had difficulty understanding. I do remember that for one surreal evening and one very long night after eating that fudge, everything in the cosmos was clear to me—strange, but clear. "Rose is a rose is a rose is a rose"? Oh, sure, I get it.

In those days, the phrase "recreational drugs" was used a lot. I don't hear it quite so much anymore, but the words give the impression that before people ran marathons and played racquetball and lifted weights in the health club, everybody sat around in their living rooms wearing tie-dyed T-shirts and smoking marijuana.

"Recreation" today means the gym, the tennis court, the Tour de France on television, and the treadmill in the basement. Forget those hippie days, forget tie-dye, forget marijuana. We have good drugs now. Those who watch the Tour de France or anything else on television know this. From migraines to menopausal mood swings to "male enhancement," each human disorder has a pharmaceutical solution. There are even pharmaceutical solutions for disorders I can't identify, because the ads on TV don't say what they are. You are supposed to "ask your doctor."

I wonder how you ask.

"Doctor, I don't know if anything is wrong with me, but could I please take some of those purple pills on TV? The ones in the ad with the naked woman under the waterfall?"

If you can get your doctor to prescribe them, these drugs promise to take care of everything. If you have high cholesterol, you can take one pill, and if you have trouble with bladder control, you can take another. If you are tired, you can take a pill instead of a nap. For erectile dysfunction, you can take Viagra, and if you are religious, you can take kosher Viagra. There are pills for hyperactivity and poor attention span in children, and there is an "adult attention deficit disorder" pill now, too, in case grown-ups feel left out.

I like drugs, and generally speaking I'm in favor of them. Without drugs several people in my family would not be alive today, including me. I take 350 mg of an anticonvulsant daily, for a seizure disorder resulting from a head injury I received at the age of twenty-seven, falling off a horse. More than thirty years later, I'm very glad this medication continues to work and grateful that the side effects are minimal.

But there are drugs and there are drugs. Some of them are life-saving, but some are questionable, some are dangerous, and many of those that are effective come with a wide range of nasty potential problems, from diarrhea to heart failure. Nonetheless, these drugs are marketed to today's television audience with the aggressive salesmanship once reserved for laundry soap and underarm deodorant.

You have to pay careful attention to the ads on television to understand that there might be negative side effects associated with any drug, because the required warnings go by very quickly and quietly, in a tone that gives the unspoken message: *We have to say this but it is not important, and only sissies listen.* Compared to the engaging footage and cheery voices in the advertisement itself, the warnings are easy to ignore.

If you don't ignore them, the possible health disasters following the words "Side effects may include . . ." are impressive. A drug to boost low energy levels following chemotherapy "may cause blood clots," meaning that some people who take this pill will follow a bout of cancer with a heart attack or a stroke. A pill for lowering cholesterol "is not for people with liver problems," and may cause "serious side effects." The job of the liver is to filter poisons in the body, so I believe we are talking about a toxic-waste overload.

To be fair, all these alarming lists and labels have arrived on the scene relatively recently, with the product labeling laws of the late 1990s. The drug companies are required to disclose any health hazards associated with their products, however slight the percentage of people affected. Because of this, even relatively innocuous products can seem alarming. A friend who was about to purchase a remedy for "watery, itchy eyes," saw that it carried warnings like "Do not take if you have heart disease, high blood pressure, or glaucoma." My helpful pharmacist tells me that this was probably just a topical antihistamine, which would require that sort of warning, but my friend decided she'd be better off letting her eyes itch.

Some people think all this labeling and listing is pretty funny. In elementary school my son and a couple of classmates performed a skit, "Side Effects," in which the narrator brightly advertised a nonexistent pharmaceutical product, then read out loud and at length the gruesome side effects. The other two children, meanwhile, were staggering around in a circle or writhing and gasping on the floor, as appropriate.

Knowing what I know from reading labels and asking questions, I still take drugs, but I try to find out what they are and what they might do to me, and I also check up on possible drug interactions. I need to know, for instance, whether an antidepressant prescribed for a short period of time, mixed with the anticonvulsant I have taken for decades, will cause me to explode. Certain combinations of drugs are like certain combinations of personalities: great to work with individually, impossible together. To forget this is easy but not wise.

I am particularly grateful for, among other drugs, the ones for depression and anxiety. I've taken some of each, and I won't hesitate to take them again if and when I need to. Anxiety medication helped me at a time when I was suddenly afraid to travel, an unusual experience for me and a real dilemma for anyone who travels frequently for work and family reasons. The antidepressant pills were a godsend during the year my mother was dying.

For many months I found it hard, somehow, just to make my way from day to day. That slow sadness, combined with an inability to work in a way that felt productive, is probably a reasonable response to having a dying mother. Still, the overall mood threatened to prevent me from doing what I had to do every day, or even from getting up in the morning. I did both, but with inexplicable difficulty and with a sense of heaviness that made me feel as if I were subject to the laws of gravity of some other and weightier planet.

Those who have never experienced depression have trouble understanding what it is. I know there are chemical explanations, but they fail to describe what I've known. Depression isn't like any other feeling I've ever had, and is not at all the same thing as sadness or grief, though depression may come along in the wake of these emotions, a gray, delayed companion.

I think of depression as a kind of influenza of the spirit, a debilitating disease that so weakens and saps the system that it becomes hard to move one's limbs. I've also thought of it as the heavy fog familiar to people living along the Maine coast and on the islands in Penobscot Bay, weather that rolls in almost imperceptibly until all at once you can't see a foot in front of you. Before you know it you are engulfed and directionless, becalmed. You can only dimly hear the steady, repeating sound of the foghorn far away, guiding other boats to harbor.

Depression is like that. As when you are sick with flu, or fogged in by weather, you can't feel the substance and meaning of the world outside yourself, so you tend to curl inward and retreat into your own small package of flesh and bones and blood and breath. These parts of you are verifiable, and from birth to death, whatever the circumstances, they give comfort. For me, the fog usually burns off in sunshine as the weather or the season changes. The flu subsides after a few days or weeks, and life continues.

I am not opposed to taking pills, but I try not to take them for conditions I can treat in other ways, not only on principle but also for economic reasons. Medication is expensive, especially over an extended period. One of the most shocking things I have heard lately about aging in America is that many older citizens on fixed incomes must choose between their prescriptions and their groceries. They can't afford both.

There is an almost-never-fail remedy for mild depression offered by a counselor-therapist friend I visit professionally several times a year, about as often as I visit the periodontist and the auto mechanic. This therapist offers valuable perspective not only on depression but on all aspects of life, and her quiet insights have helped me, and countless others, at times of trouble and sadness. She is a delightful person whose company I value for her personality, but I also trust her training and skill, and I believe that our brains and hearts deserve as much care and maintenance over time as our teeth and our automobiles. It surprises me to realize how many people deny themselves this kind of support, thinking it either improper—something you should do only if you're having a "nervous breakdown"— or prohibitively expensive. It is neither.

It is so simple and reassuring to talk for an hour now and then with a person well versed in human psychology. To do this is no more expensive—in my part of the world, anyway— than to have a couple of bitewing X-rays or a ten-thousand-mile checkup and an oil change. My last check to the garage was for more than two hundred dollars, and my last visit to the periodontist who tries valiantly to salvage my gums twice a year cost me over half that much. A visit to the counselor-therapist sets me back $75.00, and I have plenty of things to think about after I see her.

She suggests "exercise, socialization, routine, and nutrition" for mild depression, the kind of malaise that slows you down and makes you feel sad, but doesn't stop you from functioning altogether. More serious depression needs more serious treatment, and medication can help in both cases. I interpret her instructions as "move my body, see my friends, have a daily schedule, eat regularly and reasonably." It is heartening to find out how much better I feel if I take even a ten-minute walk in the morning, even on a busy day—five minutes of brisk walking away from the house, five minutes back. Following this regimen will usually pull me out of my doldrums. When it did not, I turned to drugs, even though at first I didn't like the idea of taking more pills than I was already taking. When I went to see my doctor, he assured me that an antidepressant would not interact harmfully with the seizure medication, and reminded me that this is what drugs are for: to help people.

"We couldn't do this for depression fifteen years ago," he said. "Some people never got better. There was so much suffering!" It is heartbreaking to know how widely ignored or misunderstood this condition continues to be, even now. Depression is a disease that kills those most severely afflicted, yet I wonder how many suicides have gone to their death without treatment because they, or someone else, believed they should "snap out of it," that the agony and despair they felt was "all in your mind!"

What worse place could there be for illness than the mind? If you were diseased or injured anywhere else, in the knee or in the heart, you would be rushed to a doctor for treatment. Nobody would tell you to "snap out of" degenerating joints or blocked arteries.

Despite any amount of suffering, most of the people I knew in my mother's generation would have been extremely reluctant to admit they took pills for anxiety or depression, even if they could bring themselves to do such a thing. On the other hand, many people in this same generation had no qualms whatsoever about self-medicating with alcohol.

In her remarkable book about alcohol and ancestors, *Note*

Found in a Bottle: My Life as a Drinker, Susan Cheever writes of learning from her parents at an early age about "the miraculous medicinal powers of alcohol. My mother dispensed two fingers of whiskey for stomach pain and beer for other digestive problems. Gin was an all-purpose anesthetic." However, Cheever pointed out, "When they got clinically depressed, when their adulteries caught up with them, when all the martinis in the world weren't enough to blot out the pain of their humanness, they killed themselves quietly. No one talked about it. They hanged themselves with their hats on."

I am true to my own generation. Everybody talks about almost everything but almost nobody, sadly, wears a hat. I am wary of too much alcohol and I believe in drugs—within reason.

"Why did they invent all these drugs if we're not supposed to use them, anyway?" a friend and contemporary put it. "Why can't I just take uppers and downers whenever I want? Amphetamines when I get depressed and tranquilizers when I'm anxious?" It sounded good, but I'm pretty sure that the people who do what she's describing, like the drinkers Susan Cheever remembers, tend to die young, and I'm already too old for that.

Whatever they are and whatever they are for, the drugs keep right on coming. Last night I saw two ads for sexual enhancement (one male, one female), one for a cholesterol-lowering pill, one for a treatment for adult attention deficit disorder, and one for a pill that promises to make excess weight disappear "if used with a program of healthy diet and exercise," according to the tiny message at the top of the screen. I laughed out loud at that one. With "healthy diet and exercise," all you have to do to lose weight is keep breathing, and that's still free, so far.

I have also seen articles lately in the *New York Times* and in other publications about new drugs. These are not medications to cure cancer or heart failure or even depression, but for treating conditions I have never heard of before. Perhaps these ailments have caused just as much suffering as those more familiar to me, and the people affected can finally get relief, but I sometimes can't help wondering whether the conditions existed at all before the drugs were invented.

Regardless of my views on depression as a real disease, I know how easy it is to be talked into thinking you are sick when you are actually quite healthy. Advertisers are brilliantly adept persuaders to begin with, and I remember what happened to me years ago, without advertisers, when I owned a copy of *The Merck Manual*. I finally had to get rid of it because whenever I looked through its pages I became convinced that I was sick. Whether it was the mumps or malaria, I had every single one of the symptoms of some significant disease, every single time.

A friend of mine talks with real concern about "the medicalization of human experience," a process by which more and more of the inevitable results of living our lives over time are perceived as medical disorders requiring medical responses and increasingly costly medical and pharmaceutical "treatments." I think she has a point, though I know there are miraculous drugs in our time and some of them ensure the survival of people I love, not to mention my own. I am grateful for every one of them. But the suspicion that new "diseases" are being created in order to sell new products gives me the creeps, and I resent being told that what happens to my body as it ages is something "wrong" that needs pharmaceutical fixing.

I don't want to be fixed, pharmaceutically or otherwise. I'm not any more tempted by that weight-loss pill than by the one I could take when I'm sleepy, instead of taking a nap. If I want to lose weight I can eat less and exercise more. That always works. And naps? I like naps. I plan to take more and more of them as I grow old, dozing off in my rocking chair with my spectacles slipping slowly down over the bridge of my nose and my knitting needles falling from my fingers (assuming I remember how to knit, something I haven't done for years). I think an anti-napping pill is a horrible idea!

And oh, how I wish I could banish the image conjured up in my mind by the warning that goes with the "male enhancement" ad: "If you have an erection that lasts for more than four hours, call your doctor" ("and all your friends," added a merry, wicked woman I know).

I'm looking for some balance between chemistry and philosophy, as I go on and on. I would love to grow old with as little pain and discomfort as possible, and to remain healthy for as long as I can. To that end, as I feel the need for pharmaceutical assistance, I'll surely accept it. I like drugs. I always have. Why change now?

But I don't want to be duped into buying expensive and potentially damaging drugs that I don't need, and I agree with my mother-in-law that some medications do more harm than good. Despite my own willingness to take pills for epilepsy, anxiety, depression, and diarrhea, I cannot believe that any drug manufactured or grown can produce the sense of well-being I have during those moments when, with all my aches and ailments, I am suddenly, acutely conscious of being alive: on a spring morning when the first V of wild geese flies over the farm; any time I see one of my children again after a separation; whenever I look out over the hills and pastures, or up at the stars.

I'm convinced that what we really need most to sustain us as we grow older, more than any drug on the market, is this kind of appreciative awareness, along with compassion, a sense of humor, and simple common sense. Side effects will include a certain amount of pain, a fair share of sorrow, recurring doses of discomfort great and small, and an immeasurable, priceless quantity of peace of mind.

16. Graduation Day

Our youngest son, Ben, graduated from high school in June, the last of a lively group of children who have grown up with us on this farm part or all of the time over the past thirty years. These children have included Nat's two sons, my two daughters, my late sister's son and daughter, and finally Ben, the child Nat and I had together. We raised him with the eager assistance of all the older children when they were with us, and afterward by ourselves, in the comparatively relaxed way that older parents raise their younger children.

We must seem more like Ben's grandparents than his parents to some of his friends, whose mothers and fathers are ten or even twenty years younger than we are. Ben once looked up, took the full measure of his mother and his father, and asked, "Is there *anybody* else around here under fifty?"

Not very often. The last ten years it has mostly been just one boy and two old fogies, along with the pets indoors and the farm animals outside. It gives me some comfort to know that the animals won't ever graduate and leave home, especially not those woolly dunces, the sheep.

All the same, I loved this last high school graduation. I loved seeing all these children together, some of them friends and classmates since preschool, just as they were about to step out into the world as men and women. I loved every one of the ceremonies and events I attended, and I loved most of all the small, personal moments, like the time when the headmaster asked the members of the graduating class to stand up and salute their families in the audience. Even though I was way up in the balcony of the building, squeezed in with hundreds of other mothers and fathers, and even though I had never told my child where I would be sitting during this program, he looked up, found me instantly, and blew me a kiss.

I loved seeing the four tall musicians in their caps and gowns— one boy I knew only slightly, two others I'd known since they were five years old and the fourth, my own, since the day he was born—troop up onstage to play the accompaniment for the class song: "Here I Go Again" by Whitesnake. I am not familiar with the song, and I'll never remember any of the words or even the tune, but I'll always see those four young men settling in with their instruments: one on bass, one at the keyboard, one on guitar, and our own at the drums, playing together for the last time in high school, certainly, and perhaps for the last time in their lives.

I'll remember the lump in my throat as I watched them and listened to their music, and I'll remember the way the lump was swallowed in laughter when my son told me afterward, "Yes, but I was playing with my hands. Somebody forgot to leave the drumsticks."

"Somebody"?

There were four days of graduation activities spaced out over a long weekend: a concert Friday evening, a Class Day program Saturday afternoon, a Baccalaureate Service Sunday evening, and finally the actual commencement exercises, with diplomas handed out to the graduates, on Monday morning.

Both during the Class Day program and during Commencement on Monday, prizes were awarded to the graduating seniors. There were prizes for academic achievement in every area: English, classical and foreign languages, history, science, chemistry, and mathematics. There were prizes for public speaking, poetry, music, journalism, and photography. There were technical-education and business prizes, a welding prize, a prize for outstanding achievement in culinary arts. Some of the prizes were given by former graduating classes, and there were also some named prizes: a memorial to a generous donor's late parents, or a poignant tribute to a child who would have been in this graduating class, had he or she not died.

There was a prize for "service to school and community," another for "dedication to class," and a third for "friendliness, good scholarship, and enthusiasm." As the last prizes were being awarded, I began to think that it would be nice if we parents were given prizes at graduation, too. The school could give out a Theater Arts Patience Prize to the parent who had accumulated the most hours waiting in a car late at night for a play rehearsal to finish, beyond its scheduled ending. There could be a Long Distance Driving Prize for the parent who had logged the most miles to athletic practices and other events. And how about a Mathematics Prize for any parent who was *really* able to help a child with calculus, and an English Prize for correcting the most misspellings in four years of essay assignments?

Then you could have a host of more subtle prizes, like Feeding Greatest Number of Seventeen-Year-Old Boys on Shortest Notice, or Staying Up Latest with Fifteen-Year-Old Daughter After Heartbreaking Rift with Boyfriend. Think about it. Don't parents deserve prizes, too? Haven't we earned them?

Day after day, all year long, we get out of bed early in the morning and make sure that our graduate gets out of bed, too. We should get a prize for that alone! We provide food for our children's breakfast and we entice them to eat it in spite of their morning grogginess after late-night study and/or socialization. My husband carefully prepared a slice of cantaloupe for our son each morning of his last high school semester, hoping that the juicy pink crescent and delicate scent would rouse the boy from that 6:30 A.M. somnambulist's stagger into actual consciousness before he drove to school.

Driving! There's another category. For two of his four high school years we drove him the four miles to school ourselves every day, down the long dirt road and over the winding hill into town. For the second two years we gritted our teeth at home each morning, knowing he was driving himself along the same route. His car, though not new, was sturdy, and he had taken driver's education at school and passed the test to get his license, so it only took me eight months or so to stop saying, *"Please* drive safely," every single time he left the house with the car keys in hand. Don't I get a prize for that?

And what about waiting for our high school children to drive themselves home at night? All parents know about the mortality rate in teen driving accidents nationwide; all parents fear the worst when the telephone rings after midnight. What about my friend whose son went off the road coming down a mountain in his truck, ten days after getting his driver's license? The truck rolled over several times and was totaled; the boy had his seat belt on and escaped with cuts and bruises. Still, the parents who rushed to the scene of that accident after a call from the highway patrol should have received not just a prize but a medal, a gold one.

There were many rehearsals beforehand, with hour after hour of "marching practice," as we were warned in the commencement package sent home by the school some weeks prior to graduation. The packet included a whole range of information on things like how to obtain a yearbook, what the guidelines were for attending the prom, and exactly what was considered appropriate footwear for commencement.

Our high school maintains a strict dress code for all students. The rules are carefully explained by the school handbook. Young men are required to wear dress shirts and pants, with ties "properly pulled up and visible," while young women must wear dress pants or skirts "of appropriate fit and length," and each female student who wears a blouse or top needs to ensure that it "covers midriff in all situations." Both men and women must wear their hair in "one color (naturally occurring)," and the men's hair must be "cut so that it does not touch collar and ears are visible."

I have been cutting my son's hair throughout his high school years, ever since a talented cousin showed me how to do it, because as soon as he reached early adolescence Ben refused to go back to the hairdresser where I have my own hair done, on the grounds that there were "too many ladies and too much perfume." My style with the scissors is a little casual, with an occasional design error, so it sometimes looks as if the job had been done with the sheep shears. Still, he's never lost either ear, and after the first few tries I could consistently make both of them visible without causing even minor injury. After a couple of months he barely even winced.

All the same, if his hair started to creep down over an ear on either side, violating the rules, somebody at the school always noticed. We'd address the infraction with a quick trim that very day. This is a serious dress code.

At graduation time, the seniors were all going to be capped and gowned, so I thought we parents didn't have to worry about their hair, or about how they were dressed from the ankles up. The only sartorial question in my mind that weekend concerned my graduate's feet. The normal, school-year dress code dictated "dress sandals or shoes" or "semi-formal footwear" for both men and women going to classes every day, but the commencement package told us that sandals were not acceptable footwear for the graduation ceremony.

It seemed to me that sandals and old sneakers, even less acceptable to my way of thinking, were about all we had in the house. I fretted, moreover, that our son was not taking the graduation footwear issue seriously. He was attending rehearsals and marching practice, as required, but he was also spending a lot of time with his friends, and sitting around the kitchen in the evenings talking, relaxed in his chair, sometimes absentmindedly batting at a gaudy gold-fringed Christmas ornament, studded with rhinestones, which hangs in the middle of the ceiling. We use it as a light-pull, to weight the thin cord that turns the kitchen ceiling light on and off.

This ornament actually looks like a graduation-cap tassel on steroids, and as a joke the night before graduation, somebody switched it with Ben's official tassel, a simple gold affair. When he put on his cap and turned his head, the ornament winked and glittered, shapely as a dancehall hostess from an old Western movie: Miss Lily, down at the Long Branch Saloon.

Very funny, I thought as I removed the ornament and replaced the regulation tassel on the graduation cap, but what about his feet?

"It's okay, Mom," he told me patiently when I questioned him. "I've got it covered. Everything's fine."

I knew he was probably right. Everything is almost always fine with this boy. He forgets a few things, he loses an item or two: his passport the day of an international flight, his wallet in a taxicab once—and maybe those class-song drumsticks—but generally things turn out all right. *You have to trust him on the footwear,* I told myself. *He's the one who has been going through the preparations with all the other seniors. He knows the rules and he knows the ropes. He'll have the right shoes.*

I noticed as we settled ourselves in for the final ceremony on Monday morning that the audience for this event was enormous, representing families from several surrounding towns, and that it included people of all ages and in every style of dress. There were middle-aged mothers with pearls and pocketbooks sitting next to young women in shorts pushing baby carriages. There were grandparents and siblings and aunts and uncles from across town and across the country, and there were even a few people from the other side of the world. This high school is unusual in that it is both public and private. It serves the local area through tuition arrangements with various towns, but it also has a small international-student population.

The graduating class began to march in, girls on one far side of the building, boys on the other. They moved slowly and with great dignity. All those hours of marching practice had paid off.

We were on the side closer to the girls, so I could see as they came in that these young women wore a variety of shoes. Some of them swayed along in very high, spike-heeled white pumps, looking bridal in their white caps and gowns in contrast to the green garments of their male counterparts marching along the aisle on the other side. But I saw that one girl graduate we knew was wearing little white ballet slippers, and another had sturdy Birkenstocks on her feet. So much for "inappropriate" sandals.

Over on the men's side, I couldn't see any feet at all from where I was sitting, but when the graduates sat down in their places, I could pick out the faces of some of the senior boys I knew, and I could see my own child's beloved cheek and chin, and the green cap on his head. While looking at the cap, I suddenly saw something else—the glint and flash of our kitchen Christmas ornament light-pull, not his graduation tassel.

I clutched my husband's arm. He was looking in the same direction, his eyes as wide as mine. He'd seen it, too. I wasn't dreaming. Our easygoing, absentminded youngest child, who had passed from kindergarten through twelfth grade with little difficulty of any kind, who had tied his tie every school morning for the last four years ever since the first day when his father showed him how to do it, the boy who faithfully reminded his mother when it was time to trim his hair for ear visibility, this same child was preparing to walk down the aisle and receive his diploma from his very traditional, conservative, 160-year-old high school, taking part in what the handbook calls "a distinguished procession of men and women," with Miss Lily swaying and sashaying and glittering like a diamond necklace from his graduation cap.

I stared over at my son, who did not look back at me, though his gaze swept once in our direction, his eyes innocent and his expression sober, deadpan. Anyone looking at his face would think he was awed by the solemnity of the occasion. But when his head turned to face the stage, I saw a little twinkle of rhinestones, and I sank down in my folding chair.

Was there a prize for having a child expelled from high school at the closest possible moment to graduation?

Graduation ceremonies can seem very long, with all the speeches and all the prizes until finally, at the very end, the graduates come up one by one to receive their diplomas and to have their pictures taken with the person who presents them, in this case the president of the school's board of trustees. The graduates come up toward the front in alternating rows, first a row from the girls' side, then a row of boys, with two representatives from next year's graduating class acting as marshals to indicate when each row should rise and move forward to the side of the stage to wait until their individual names are called.

Our son's last name begins with "T," which put him toward the very end of the group of graduating seniors, so under normal circumstances we might have found it a lengthy and tedious wait before we saw our child go up the steps and across the stage to receive his diploma, shake hands, and have his picture taken. In this case, the minutes flew by all too quickly. We sat at the edge of our seats, eyes darting nervously around, looking for the Graduation Police to arrive and bust our kid during the last twenty minutes of his high school career.

But nothing happened.

When it was Ben's turn to graduate, he walked up the steps and across the stage, received his diploma, shook hands with the president of the board of trustees, and posed for the photographer, sober as a judge and solemn as an owl, with Miss Lily dancing and glittering three inches from his nose. I have the photograph in front of me as I write, and to my eyes, anyway, it is spectacular.

But nobody else seemed to see it. Maybe the Graduation Police were asleep that day, or maybe they decided to overlook a minor misdeed on a beautiful morning. Or maybe, and I think this is the most likely explanation, nobody but us noticed that outrageous, outsized, outlaw gold tassel. While we gripped our seats and felt our hearts pound, with our eyes riveted on our child, all the other mothers and fathers were doing exactly the same thing, looking only at their children. Why would they notice anyone else? The students were concerned with getting through this ceremony at long last and then going on to the postgraduation celebrations with their friends. The speakers were concentrating on delivering their speeches, the headmaster and the faculty members were focused on completing their final tasks for yet another graduating class at this high school, in yet another year. Nobody was looking at tassels, except for Nat and me.

Sometimes, though, I think this tassel is magic and invisible, because even now if I show the graduation photograph to friends and ask if they see anything odd about it, what they notice is Ben's somber expression, or the pretty face of the president of the board of trustees ("Who's *that?*). One person remarked that the background image of an Aladdin-style lamp, on the school banner behind Ben's head, made it look as if he had moose horns growing out of his cap—but nobody mentioned the tassel, not one person. It has *rhinestones* all over it. I just don't understand.

The ceremony ended. The graduates rose and were applauded by the audience. They filed out followed by the faculty, the speakers, and honored guests. The audience began to mill around and gather itself to move toward the door. Nat and I got up from our seats a little shakily, and joined the crowd.

Didn't we deserve a prize for what we had just been through? We did. I had absolutely no doubt in my mind about that. And we got one, too. There was our prize, just as impossibly priceless as all the others before him, all the graduates who have left our home and remain in our hearts and lives. He was walking across the grass toward his parents with his diploma in hand, capped and gowned and tasseled and grinning—ours, oh so unmistakably ours, on graduation day.

17. Living with the Dog

It has occurred to me that I am currently spending my days in much the same living situation I knew thirty-five years ago. At that time I had just gotten married. I had left behind my parents' household and my identity as a child of their family, but I did not yet have children of my own. Now as then, I live in a very small family unit: two people and a dog.

When a couple lives with a dog and no other human beings, little by little the dog becomes a third person in the minds of the two humans. They start to behave differently toward, and in reference to, the animal. The dog still behaves like a dog, though it sometimes looks confused.

I first heard of this phenomenon many years ago when friends of my mother's came with their pet to visit her for afternoon tea. This happened in the French-speaking part of Switzerland, and the dog's name was Fripon, which according to my French dictionary means "little rogue" or "rascal."

During the few hours these two ladies were with her, my mother said, she learned about Fripon's diet, bowel movements, and likes and dislikes in more detail than was necessary, and there was a rich array of French cooing noises and indulgent phrases spread over the conversation like marmalade on toast:

"Oooh, Fripon, qu'est-ce que tu fais là?"

The attention lavished upon this small creature was impressive, but the dog took it all in stride and spent the whole time casting plaintive, nobody-ever-feeds-me looks first at my mother and then toward the fruit pastries from the *patisserie* in the nearby town of Vevey. Fripon was nobody's fool.

Later in her life my mother fell victim to the same affliction. During the first bout of it my father was still living, and he fell, too. I think of this as the Small Dog syndrome. After many years of owning big, bouncing, hearty family dogs, dogs compatible with children and bicycles and running to catch the school bus, some couples decide to change their canine habits entirely. They switch from being Big Dog people to being Small Dog people.

When the final noble German shepherd has passed away, after the sad demise of the last loyal Labrador or goofy golden retriever, there is a decent pause to mark the ending of an era. Then, in a former Big Dog family, there appears a Small Dog: dachshund, Norwich terrier, West Highland white. No, no, he doesn't yip, and she would never bite your ankles—isn't that right, Fripon?

Choosing a name for the first post-family Small Dog is an elaborate process, not unlike choosing a name for a first baby, possibly a first baby in a royal family. My mother's first Small Dog, a blackish salt-and-pepper-haired cairn terrier, was ultimately named Brenna, which means "raven maid" in Gaelic or Celtic or whichever language cairn terriers speak. There were several other names in contention, all of them worthy of a Small Dog princess, none of which I can recall. I don't think the dog knew her name anyway, because my parents so often absentmindedly called her by names belonging to their children.

My name was the one I heard used most often for the dog, I suppose because I had been the last child to leave the household.

It was a real shock to come home from college for a weekend during my freshman year, feeling free and sophisticated, only to hear my father thunder at me, "Reeve! IN A CORNER!"

The dog was begging at my father's knee under the tea table, and the "corner" was a designated spot beneath the big desk by the window in the living room.

The dog went, and I almost went with her.

When I stopped trembling, I was as irritated as I was amused. It was fun to catch my father red-handed in an embarrassing error. This rarely happened, and even when it did, he wouldn't admit it. But what could he do in this case? He laughed, and I laughed, too, though I was inwardly indignant. How was it possible that my own father could mistake that pint-sized ambulating carpet for *me,* his beloved child?

Now I know how it happens. My daughter Susannah, the one with the long blonde hair, left home fifteen years ago or so for boarding school and then college and finally California, where she now lives. Our yellow Lab, Elsa, is seven years old, with a lovely golden coat. She has gentle brown eyes, not blue ones, and she has four feet and a tail. Elsa and Susannah have rarely been under the same roof. But nonetheless, every so often, guess what I say when I call the dog?

"Here, Susannah!"

But I still think this is much more understandable than it was in my father's case all those years ago. Elsa and Susannah are both blondes, for one thing, although one is a golden Lab and the other a golden girl. They are both very affectionate and very intelligent. One of them has learned to make pirogies from a recipe in her fiancé's family, the other is really good at catching frogs. The confusion is understandable, isn't it?

The odd thing about this is that our last child to leave home was not Susannah, but Ben. I'm surprised that I don't use his name rather than his sister's, when I get absentminded. I'm aware that the dog and the daughter are female and Ben is a boy, but if you're going to confuse species, then gender confusion is a mere quibble.

Elsa even belongs to Ben, technically. She came into his life and ours in the autumn of 1999, when he was in seventh grade and she was a two-month-old puppy. The dog has been right here on the farm ever since, though the boy keeps leaving for longer and longer stretches of time. I guess catching frogs just isn't good enough for some people.

Because Elsa looked like a little lion cub when she was small, she was named for the lioness in Joy Adamson's book *Born Free*. Lions belong to the cat family, and Labrador retrievers to the dog family, which may explain the reproachful looks Elsa directs our way when we call her: *I still don't believe this! You named me for an oversized cat?*

I may be wrong about this, because I don't think dogs listen too closely to what people are saying. Most of it is so senseless and repetitive. Aside from the compliments, "What a good dog!" and the commands "Sit," "Stay," and "IN A CORNER!" no response is required. I remember a cartoon I saw twenty years ago in which a dog sits, bleary-eyed, in front of a man wagging an admonitory finger and reprimanding his pet at great length. The caption goes something like, *"Blah blah blah blah blah blah blah* Bad Dog *blah blah blah blah blah* Good Dog *blah blah blah blah blah blah."*

Who wants to listen to all that blather? I'm sure that's why dogs are dozing so much of the time. Human conversation bores them to sleep.

But people go right on talking to their dogs anyway. At my house a lot of the talk occurs in the kitchen near the door to the porch, the door through which Elsa likes to go in and out (and in and out and in and out) all day long. I have an inane daily habit of asking her about this behavior.

"What do you see out there, Elsa?"

"What are you barking at?"

She responds by thumping her tail on the floor, and since I don't speak tail-thump, I don't learn much, though I'd actually like to know the answers to my questions. What *is* all that early-morning barking about? Is it directed at something or somebody? Or is it just a general announcement, like the crowing of the roosters at dawn? *It's daytime, and I'm here!*

Nat thinks it's all a big bluff. Elsa is trying to sound like a much more formidable dog than the surrounding wildlife knows she really is. They remember that she once ran out to confront a deer under the apple tree, but when the deer turned toward her she whirled and ran back toward the house as fast as she could go, with the deer in full pursuit. This is a dog who was chased by a deer in her own driveway. We were witnesses, but we try not to mention it when she is in the room.

My husband does not ask the dog questions the way I do. Instead he likes to talk to her about upcoming shared activities: "That's right! We're going out to feed the sheep / stack wood / shovel manure!" He speaks so enthusiastically and with such promise of fun and joy in his voice that the dog begins to bounce and yelp in anticipation. *Yippee! Manure!*

At other times he talks very softly, with admiration and love, for instance when she is sitting on the old sofa looking out the window at the fields and sky, in her Noble Dog pose.

"You are the best," Nat says then. "You are the most beautiful, wise, intelligent, sensitive dog on earth." That is a direct quote from five minutes ago. I took notes.

Thump-thump, goes the tail on the sofa. The dog has her own sofa now. Why not? Nobody else was using it. Lately she has been known to creep up onto other pieces of furniture as well: one really comfortable armchair, and our bed. I don't know how it happened. Didn't we once have a Dog Bed? And rules? Wasn't there a crate, before that, with blankets and dog toys and bones, where the puppy was trained to sleep at night? How did we end up with a full-sized Labrador retriever sleeping at, and on, our feet?

I can't remember how it all came about, but now I sleep very carefully, in a kind of foreshortened curve, with my legs carefully arranged so as not to disturb the dog. My husband may complain grumpily, "Elsa, would you *please* move over?" if she stretches out too far in his direction, but he is just as likely to be talking to her adoringly when I come into the bedroom after I've brushed my teeth at night. There is my beloved mate, crooning and fondling the dog's ears, his head on his own pillow, her head on mine. At these times I have to make it clear to both of them that there's only one head allowed in that particular spot, and it isn't the one that eats chicken guts.

All the same, day or night, the companionship of a dog is a wonderful thing. The rugs and the furniture in our house may be hairier than they are in most other people's homes, and some of the conversations you overhear don't make a lot of sense, especially when Nat is talking into the empty air about sheep manure and red squirrels.

There is absolutely nothing to compare with sitting on the porch in the sunshine in early spring, sipping a mug of hot coffee and looking out over the hills to the tree line, with a green haze of buds about to burst open, birds singing in nearby branches, and my dog lying on the porch beside me, chewing on one of those things dogs like to chew on. It might be a dog biscuit or a bone or a piece of wood, or maybe an old stalk of brussels sprouts from the garden, or maybe something else.

Reeve Lindbergh

Once when I looked down at Elsa on just such an occasion I caught a sunlit glimpse of her lovely yellow Labrador profile as she was gently chewing, and then spotted the long skinny line of a rodent's tail protruding from the end of her mouth, sort of like a toothpick.

I knew what she and I were both thinking at that moment: it doesn't get any better than this.

18. *Vanity, Gravity, Levity*

I've often hoped that as I advanced in years I would also advance as a human being, "every day, in every way, getting better and better," as the old saying goes. I've even secretly wished that as a very old lady I might become a truly saintly individual, like one lovely old woman I used to know. She was almost incandescent with goodness, having spent a selfless life helping others and never uttering an unkind word about anybody. She had a beautiful face, and beautiful hands softened by innocent old-fashioned lotions that smelled like roses, and yet she seemed to be entirely without vanity.

I've also thought it could be interesting to go in the opposite direction and turn into a little old Holy Terror. I've known a couple of those, too.

So far, though, I just seem to continue being me, the same person I was at twelve and at fifty. If sainthood or deviltry is my destiny, then destiny is taking its own sweet time, especially in the "getting better" department. Though I try to be friendly and polite and generous and thoughtful, as my mother instructed her children to be, I have many faults. I know I'm not selfless, for one thing.

At sixty I'm just as self-indulgent as I ever was, possibly more so. I put extra butter on my English muffins, I paint my toenails bright red in winter even though nobody can see them but me, and at certain times you will find me lying on my bed reading a book when I should be sitting at my desk writing one. I try not to utter unkind words, often because they generate a kind of trouble that is both painful and time-consuming. But never? How I wish that were true!

Vanity may be less of a problem than it was forty years ago, though I can't take much credit for that. At this age, what choice do I have? When my late sister, Anne, turned fifty she told me, "After a certain age, there's only so good you can look." Anne was a beautiful woman all her life, so to hear her say this made me smile, but I understood what she meant. One reaches a time in life when the attempt to look gorgeous requires an effort greater than any results it can possibly produce. That's when it makes sense to make friends with reality.

I find that I don't mind looking at my face in the mirror anymore, except maybe in the middle of the night—that can be scary. I've "grown accustomed to my face," to paraphrase the song Professor Higgins sings about Eliza Doolittle in *My Fair Lady*. I'm not only accustomed to my face, but I've also become quite fond of it. This is a very different feeling from the one I had at twenty or thirty or even forty, when I worried constantly about its faults and flaws. Maybe I care less now than I did then about how I look to other people, or maybe I know from long experience that most people ignore *our* imperfections because they are concentrating upon *theirs*.

Furthermore, I no longer have the good eyesight and steady hands to do what I did every single morning when I was twenty. I would stand in front of the bathroom mirror trying to hold an eyelid still with one hand while brushing eye shadow on it and then painting a tiny stripe of eyeliner along the lower part, just above the eyelashes, with the other. This was a complex process, especially for a left-handed person with questionable fine motor skills. I would find myself in a complicated self-hug, elbows criss-crossing over my chest like the gesture that went with a song we used to sing in summer camp in the fifties:

> *I love myself. I think I'm grand!*
> *I sit in the movies and I hold my hand.*
> *I wrap myself in a warm embrace,*
> *And if I get fresh, I slap my face!*

After applying the eyeliner I would take out a tube of mascara and cover my lashes languorously with the little brushy liquid-coated wand, blotting the dark residue with Kleenex in the hope that the stuff would not all be transferred, as it usually was by the first blink after application, to my upper cheek. Mascara provided less glamour than I hoped for, leaving me as it so often did with that sleep-deprived raccoon look.

The place where the mascara once ended up is now webbed with what the cosmetics people call "the appearance of wrinkles." I am aware that it's the *reality* of wrinkles. I don't care what they tell you on TV. But I also like to think of it as the appearance of ancestors. Sometimes when I look at my face in the mirror now, due to the passage of time and the forces of gravity, I can see my mother's face and even my grandmother's face looking back at me: blue eyes, wrinkles, glasses, and all. It is a very friendly family reflection.

I mention the glasses because I rarely wear them in the bath-room, what with the potential for splattering toothpaste on the lenses, stepping on them in the shower, and/or absentmindedly flushing them down the toilet. When I say I don't mind looking at my face in the mirror anymore, part of the reason may be that I can't see it. That is not such a bad thing, either. I have often felt that the inevitable gradual failing of our eyesight over the years is

God's plan to help us let go of vanity. By the time you don't want to look at your face, you can't see it anyway—perfect solution.

I may feel a nostalgic recognition and a sweet yearning for those long-gone wrinkly faces I find in the mirror, like the feeling I have if I visit a house I knew intimately in childhood. But the truth is that my feminine forbears did not surrender to their own wrinkled landscapes without a fight, and neither will I. I still make an effort, at least "in public," which means in places where the majority of other women wear real makeup, like Texas.

Like my mother before me, I have some pink stuff that I put on my cheeks and some red stuff that I put on my lips (not to mention the toenail polish) and I even have a little compact, with a remnant of face powder in an undetermined color, the label long gone. That's as far as I am willing to go, even if I get to Houston.

Real makeup doesn't work for me. It never did. The mascara was bad, but other things were worse. I couldn't use the gooey stuff that came out of bottles labeled "Foundation," which was applied to the face like a primer coat in house painting, before other applications went on with wands and brushes. "Foundation" made my skin itch and gave me claustrophobia, probably because in earlier years I was susceptible to poison ivy, and spent many spring and summer days and nights covered in pink, flaking calamine lotion. As medicine, it was effective, but it was the makeup from hell.

There are thousands of women of high intelligence, warm heart, and fine character for whom makeup is an art mastered early in life and so essential to one's daily wardrobe that it would be as unacceptable to leave home without it as it would be to walk out the front door stark naked. Most of these women, at least the ones I know, live in states where they would not catch cold if they did go forth into the world naked. Makeup, like the mint julep, is a Southern thing, though not exclusively.

Last summer a friend of mine here in Vermont miraculously survived a terrible car accident. The vehicle was destroyed, but her husband escaped with bumps and bruises and she felt "lucky" to come out of the experience with only a badly broken right arm. It was not an easy time. When some of us stopped by a few days after the accident, she was thankful to be alive, and was managing pretty well under the circumstances. We had been most worried about the pain in her body and the state of her mind, but she told us that another woman had telephoned her, very distressed to hear her news, with only one pressing concern:

"How will you put on your makeup?"

My friend was just beginning to absorb the daily difficulty of brushing her teeth, getting her clothes on, and answering the telephone one-handed, so she found herself unable to answer.

I'm not saying that vanity is all bad. Millions of women—and men, too, these days—work hard to counteract the effects of aging. Their dedication provides jobs and profits for the cosmetics industry and enriches plastic surgeons all over the world. It bolsters sagging economies while lifting drooping faces and other body parts. Some people, including actors who depend upon youthful good looks for the continuation of their careers, may succeed through repeated surgery in making themselves look younger than they really are, at least for a while. Other people usually only make themselves look hazardous, because their skin is stretched so tightly over their bones that it looks to an observer as if the whole face might split open at any moment like an overripe pea pod and spill its contents.

No matter how good the results of plastic surgery may be, they don't last forever. Everyone who gets old will look old, someday. Most of us retreat from the battle somewhere along the line, leave vanity to those who enjoy it, and amuse ourselves in other ways.

For those aging women who have lived in the country too

long, or have just lived too long to remember the knack of putting on makeup, and for those hopeless fashion duds like me who never got the hang of it in the first place and had creepy calamine lotion claustrophobia, there is another way to cheer your days, brighten your appearance, and enhance those glimpses of yourself in the mirror or in store windows that you can't avoid—and you know you can't avoid them all.

Ladies, I give you *Accessories!* Hats, scarves, earrings, pins, and socks, the brighter the better, especially the socks.

I have cheered myself through two weeks of rainy weather and a set of abnormal test results, very scary ones, simply by wearing colorful socks. I have a large collection. My socks are of various colors and motifs, and may be decorated with anything from white sheep on neon-green fabric to red hot peppers against a sophisticated black wool blend. Where I live there is a "Vermont Sock Lady," too, an entrepreneurial genius who understands the power of footwear. She has created a line of vibrant hosiery, every single sock a little different from every other, in irresistible colors and one-of-a-kind patterns. She markets these with the inspiring thought: "Life Is Too Short For Matching Socks."

This is true, in the greater scheme of things. However, most of us live not in greater schemes but in smaller ones, and prevailing opinion in our society dictates that matching socks are essential: nobody ever got elected to public office or became a senior partner without matching socks. One has to muster a good deal of energy and fearlessness to buck the trend. Interestingly, this kind of mustering is much easier at sixty than it was at nineteen. As Bette Davis famously told us, "Old age ain't no place for sissies."

Hats are helpful accessories, too, though my opinion is that women who wear hats well need to have a flair for it. Hat wearing can easily go over the edge, as reflected by the Red Hat societies that have sprung up around the country recently. These are organizations of women of a certain age who have taken to putting on crimson hats of all shapes and sizes, and gathering in Red Hat groups, like flocks of tufted titmice. The inspiration for this behavior is a poem by Jenny Joseph called "When I Am an Old Woman I Shall Wear Purple," though I read an article in which the poet herself denied all responsibility for the Red Hat craze. I had a sense when I first read it that the poem was about her own plans for an old age in which she would do all the things she had been told she shouldn't throughout her life, like wearing purple "with a red hat which doesn't go, and doesn't suit me" and learning to spit—becoming a Holy Terror, in other words.

There is nothing wrong with red hats, or with hats of any shade, shape, or dimension. I have one elegant and charming female friend, several decades older than I (imagine that!), who was born with the instinctive style and good fashion sense to wear hats well. This is not a characteristic given to just anybody, but a gift bestowed upon a lucky few by some good fairy at birth, and it lasts a lifetime. The girl who stood on a platform with a smart little black beret perched aslant on her head and waved to a soldier leaving on a troop train in 1942 is the same white-haired woman with the stunning wide-brimmed confection you notice at her granddaughter's summer wedding in the twenty-first century.

My mother wore scarves when I knew her, not hats. She liked to have "something silky at the throat," and said she did this to soften the look of an aging neck as well as to complement whatever she was wearing. Often there was a simple gold or silver pin fastened to the scarf, fashioned in the form of a shell or a tiny, bare tree branch, or a heart.

Along with the scarves, and long before Jenny Joseph wrote her poem, my mother wore purple, but gently. She called it "lavender." I always think of her in this color, though she wore others. She had lavender trousers and a lavender sweater, and once I think there was a full-length lavender winter coat, for her days in New York City, but I might be making this up, or remembering one my sister, Anne, wore in the same era, of a slightly different color.

Anne and I inevitably acquired the lavender habit ourselves. Like the lifelong trait of writing down impressions and insights, wearing lavender was something so characteristic of our mother that it must have seeped into her daughters' lives through heredity or by simple osmosis. I hardly noticed our color preference until one summer day here in Vermont. My sister arrived with her children at the public beach on Harvey's Lake, in West Barnet. (This is a body of water once explored by Jacques Cousteau, I've been told many times, and I believe it, but I have never found out when this happened, or why.) I was already at the lake with a close friend and our own young children, who were swimming and splashing together at the water's edge. My friend looked up as Anne arrived, then grinned at her and groaned, "Oh, no—not another Lindbergh in lavender!"

I should also confess my disastrous youthful excursions into lavender eye shadow when I was twenty, but nothing will make me reveal what I looked like wearing the white lipstick I applied to my mouth at the same time. What was I thinking? I'm so glad I don't remember.

I don't do that anymore. I don't do anything, really, except for the pink stuff and the red stuff, and the toenail polish. I don't know whether I have truly shed my vanity or whether I have just acquired laziness along with the myopia, but life is very comfortable this way, whichever it is.

On my sixtieth birthday, however, it occurred to me that I don't even know what the vanity options *are* for people my age. I thought I should do a little research, so I went to our largest local pharmacy, bought a notebook and a pencil, and went up and down the aisles in the "beauty" section and took notes. I didn't actually purchase any products useful to my vanity or even to my well-being, but I did go home and write a little poem:

> Promises, Promises . . . or, What I Did
> On My Sixtieth Birthday
>
> *When I turned sixty*
> *I found in the store*
> *A world of temptations*
> *For girls of three score.*
>
> *Definers for eyebrows*
> *And liners for pants*
> *And remedies made*
> *From obscure jungle plants.*
>
> *Pills for our ills,*
> *For good moods, for good sex,*
> *Supports for our feet*
> *And our backs and our necks.*
>
> *Glamorous hair dyes*
> *Row upon row*
> *To transform our tresses*
> *To auburn from snow.*
>
> *And oh, the cosmetics!*
> *The powders! The creams!*
> *They promise results*
> *From our farthest-fetched dreams.*
>
> *Here is what it says they'll do.*
> *How can I resist this stuff? Can you?*
> *They won't fade or cake or streak.*
> *We'll look younger in a week.*

With our Anti-Wrinkling Serum,
We who have Fine Lines won't fearum.
No, we'll be Regenerating:
Moistly, Actively Hydrating!
With these products we'll be using,
We won't age. We'll be Diffusing.
We'll be dancing, we'll be prancing
While De-Crinkling and Enhancing
(No one's footsteps could be dragging
While her face cream's Anti-Sagging).

A world of temptations,
Yet I could not choose
From all of these things
Even one I would use.

I declined to be eye-lined,
Hydrated, Enhanced,
Supported for sex, or by socks,
Or in pants.

I left the store happy, though.
Isn't that funny?
I'm learning, at sixty,
How NOT to spend money.

I'm learning other things, too. I'm learning that however much I would like to be transformed into a saintly old woman, or a devilish one, I probably won't be. I'll remain the person I am, only older, and in getting older I will acquire some aches and ills along with some sorrows and—yes!—some joys, like the joy of watching my daughter try on her wedding dress, and the joy of holding grandchildren in my arms. I am learning that even though I might yearn to stay alive and vigorously healthy for another sixty years, that, too, is unlikely. The span of years I can look forward to is contracting as the days behind me accumulate, and maybe that is why old people are said to "live in the past." The past must seem so generous, with its rich accumulation of days and experiences, unlike the constrained and sometimes painful present, or the limited and unpromising future.

But doesn't the idea of limitation exist in the imagination, like the notion that purple eye shadow and white lipstick will really confer glamour and sophistication? Or the idea that face cream of any variety, at any price, will really prevent wrinkles? I know that aches and sorrows will come with old age, but I have had plenty of aches and sorrows already. It isn't a huge surprise to me that others are in store. Some of my own sorrows have been with me for so long, sweet and sad companions, that they are old friends. Like the wrinkles on my face. I live with them every day, and they don't scare me anymore.

There is no cosmetic remedy for the passing of time, but it is possible to stop now and then, physically and mentally, for just long enough to experience the world around me and the world within me at any given moment, to pause and acknowledge, even for a few seconds, exactly where I am and what I see and how it feels to be here, only that. It seems so simple it's almost ridiculous, but in such moments I find it is impossible to be afraid. I understand at the age of sixty, at least for a blessed instant now and then, that all I really can do with the rest of my life is to laugh at myself when laughter is called for, weep when I need to, and feel all of it, every bit of it, as much as I can for as long as I can. So that's what I think I'll do.

19. The Oldest Unwed
Mother in Caledonia County

Every time I feel an attack of moral outrage coming on, I walk over to the family bulletin board. There among the old dog tags and curling photographs and spare keys and cards for upcoming dental appointments, I see a little blue-and-white identification pin, the kind of thing that might have been worn by a nurse or a medical technician at our local hospital twenty years ago, before they started wearing photo ID badges. It has these words neatly etched in it: "Oldest Unwed Mother in Caledonia County."

A friend of mine gave it to me as a joke after I had referred to myself this way during my last pregnancy, which coincided with a tricky legal period of my otherwise relatively respectable life. My first marriage was not exactly over and my second one had not exactly started, but the child of this second marriage was well on the way. I was forty-one years old, and there you have it.

If I search my conscience, I am a little bit embarrassed about this part of my past, but not terribly embarrassed, I confess. We live in an age when such things happen without tremendous societal repercussions. Besides, as my brothers and my sister and I used to say during our childhood if confronted by discovered misdeeds, "It was a long time ago, Father."

I try to be fair-minded, to consider my own shortcomings before judging another person's actions or criticizing somebody else's way of life. A tolerant perspective comes easily for me most of the time, but not always, which brings me to another story.

Thirty years after my father's death, and about two and a half years after my mother had passed away, I learned that my father had secret families in Europe: three of them. I had brothers and sisters I had never known about, two girls and five boys, living in several different countries on another continent. My father, who traveled constantly for as long as I knew him, had produced these children during the later part of his life, when he was between fifty-five and sixty-five years old. His European children were a generation younger than his American offspring. (I was the youngest child in his American family, having been born in 1945, when he was forty-three).

During all the years when he was the stern arbiter of moral and ethical conduct in our family, he had been leading another life, living according to a whole different set of standards from those he had taught to me.

At first I couldn't believe it.

I felt nothing but indignation at the news. What? Yet another weird "Lindbergh" story? Another "Pretender" claiming to be the first of my parent's children, Charles, who died as a result of the notorious kidnapping in 1932? There have been as many as fifty of these claimants, though in recent years I have only been hearing from three of them. Or was it one more twist in the "Lindbergh as Nazi" story, because of my father's isolationist views and speeches before the Second World War? Another resurrection of ancient stories in lives long over?

Please! The man has been dead for three decades. Why not let him rest in peace?

Then, when the story about the secret families turned out to be true, I became furiously angry, as angry as I have ever been in my life. I was not angry with my "new," living relatives, no more to blame for the circumstances of their birth than I am, but with my long-dead father. I raged against his duplicitous character, his personal conduct, the years of deception and hypocrisy.

My father was many things to many people. In his youth, as a result of a remarkably successful, well-planned aviation adventure, he had been hailed as a hero by adoring crowds all over the world. In middle age he took a political position that left him open to criticism for the rest of his days. But privately, as a father, he had lectured me about moral and ethical behavior, and that was all I could think about.

"Don't do anything that cheapens life," he had said, and I tried to follow this piece of advice even though I wasn't quite sure what it meant. Now, with the secret families revealed, I thought his advice was meaningless, his teachings false, and *his* life cheap.

What really drove me crazy, the way one small thing will drive you crazy when something big happens, was that he had once written a chastising letter to my sister when she was at college. It was an angry letter, a searing page of paternal moralizing, telling her that she had too many boyfriends, and doing it in a cruel way, hinting at her potential "promiscuity," a strange word for a father to use. After my sister died of cancer in 1993 her daughter found the letter. Anne had saved it for thirty years.

And she died before she knew about his own behavior. Oh, I was angry!

My anger was all-consuming, a satisfyingly fiery and righteous rage, very comforting while it lasted. Unfortunately it lasted, in full force, for only about a month.

On Friday, August 8, 2003, two weeks after learning the news about my father's life in Europe, I wrote this in my journal:

. . . this story reflects absolutely Byzantine layers of deception on the part of our shared father. These children did not even know who he was! He used a pseudonym with them (To protect them, perhaps? To protect himself, absolutely!) . . .

On August 25 I was still at it:

. . . I am truly incensed and sickened . . .

On the 26th, the anniversary of his death, I wrote more quietly, but I remember the bitterness I felt:

. . . Twenty-nine years ago today my father died. At his death, it seems, several of his children did not even know his name.

Anger, bitterness, outrage, all were with me for a while. Then, one by one, they went away. I can still bring any of them back if I try, but I can't maintain the feelings for long. This I find very interesting.

I keep a journal for many reasons, but the most important one is that I want to be as honest with myself as possible. I think it is very hard to be absolutely honest with oneself, especially if words come easily. Before I write, I have to ask myself what I think, and if the answer comes too quickly I have to stop and ask again—No, what do I *really* think? Words have always served me as a way of organizing my responses to life, which doesn't necessarily mean that my words have always reflected the truth, not even to me. But I would like to write more and more truthfully as I grow older. That means I have to write with great care, I find, and more slowly.

I think my tendency is to edit thoughts and feelings, and then to form my awareness and memory from the edited version, so that what happens in my life is always acceptable through language: "I was devastated," "I was furious," "I was overjoyed," "I was deeply moved," "I was grateful." There. It has been described. It's finished. It's over. Thank goodness. Now I can go on with my life.

But if I am honest I have to admit that my strong emotions are rarely if ever "finished" and that when I feel them, I feel many at the same time, including some I can't or don't dare to express: *Aha! I always thought my father was crazy! This proves it! Or even, Gosh! No wonder he was such a pain in the ass!*

I remember my father as a deeply intelligent and incredibly energetic man, a man of warmth and humor and charm and a kind of old-fashioned shy courtesy that I always attributed to his Midwestern upbringing. I also remember my father as the most infuriatingly impossible human being I have ever known: an angry, restless, opinionated perfectionist, never able to be still for any length of time, so obsessed with his own ideas and concerns that when he was at home his very presence alternately crowded and startled everyone else in the family, even the dog.

All these decades after his death, when I learned that there were three women in my father's life besides my mother, one of my first thoughts was that this arrangement made a certain kind of sense. No one woman could possibly have lived with him all the time.

The story of the secret families had me raging, thinking, writing, and trying to be honest for about a month. Then something changed. On September 4, 2003, I wrote only one sentence in my journal: *"God help me, I'm beginning to get used to this!"* It is extraordinary how quickly one can absorb new information, whatever it is. I still can't come to a satisfactory conclusion about my father's secret life; I still feel surges of anger and pain, but not often. Over the months and years, familiarity overcame shock, and what was once an outrage became another condition of life. By now, if I'm not "over" the discovery that my father had another life, I am at least used to it.

I cannot hang on to moral outrage for very long anyway, however justified it may seem. So much that goes on in the world is so terrible to contemplate that any family's scandals and sorrows eventually have to be seen in perspective. Besides, moral outrage is no fun. It devours time, monopolizes conversation, and bores other people to tears.

For me the emotions wore themselves out, and reason began to creep into my thinking. However outrageous I may think it, I cannot change the truth of the past, and as time goes on I realize that I have very little to complain about. The only damage I've sustained through these discoveries about my father is in the realm of the imagination. My old ideas about my personal world are altered. My family is not exactly as I had thought. It is different.

This certainly is not the first or the worst instance of a change in my personal world. There have been others much more painful. The illnesses and deaths of my infant son and my sister, the long, slow dying of my mother, these changed the landscape of my life profoundly, much more than any revelation about my father's history can ever do.

Thinking about him these days, I am aware that ideas about my father distorted his life from the time of his famous flight in 1927. At that moment in history he became a public figure, a subject of millions of photographs, a magnet for ideas: about the aviator, about the man—"a boy," they called him—about aviation, about the nature of heroes, about the character of the United States itself. In the minds of those people who know him historically but did not know him personally, my father exists as a kind of frozen image. There are no relationships involved, and regardless of anything that may be revealed about him, the image does not change.

For me it is more difficult. From the moment of the discovery that he had other families, I knew that if I tried to look for my father again in the light of this new information, I would not find him in public images. I would have to look somewhere else. At the same time I was aware that my brothers and sisters on two continents were trying to raise their children and live their lives and come to terms with these revelations, as I was. Three of these were people I had known and loved for my whole life. The others were strangers, yet as closely related to me as my daughter Susannah is to my son, Ben.

I wanted to know them.

Many of us in the families wanted to know one another, but it was difficult to make the first, quiet connections because of publicity. It was astonishing to me that so much fuss was being made over the private life of a dead aviator who had stopped making news thirty years ago. In the summer of 2003, when the story about my father's other children appeared in the European media, we in his American family were asked to comment immediately, before we had absorbed the news. Here in Vermont I had calls from the *New York Times, People* magazine, and several representatives of foreign newspapers and television stations.

One European correspondent telephoned my home when I was away. My son answered the phone, listened in baffled silence to a barrage of questions in a foreign accent, and handed the phone to his father. Nat knew very little about the rumors from Europe at the time, but he has fielded many a strange "Lindbergh" phone call over the years, from overeager newspaper reporters, representatives of one or the other of the "Pretenders," or an occasional legitimate, if strange, historical researcher. As soon as he could get a word in, he told the caller, "This is ridiculous!" and hung up.

Soon a newspaper article appeared in this country, claiming that I had told a foreign journalist that the reports of my father's other families were "ridiculous." In fact I had not spoken to any media representative at all, about anything. Other family members in the U.S. were besieged with questions as well. We decided to issue a family statement. I memorized it, and I've also pinned it up on the same bulletin board that holds the "Oldest Unwed Mother" pin, for reference. It goes like this:

> The Lindbergh family is treating this situation as a private matter, and has taken steps to open personal channels of communication, with sensitivity to all concerned.

What that really means, I think, is something like

> We don't know any more than you do, but we're trying to figure this out while causing as little pain as possible.

Issuing a statement for the media was the best thing we could think to do with the information we had at the time. Later, however, we were able to open those "personal channels."

It was my brother Scott, driving through France, who attended the first, very secret meeting between families. Scott lives in Brazil but spends a lot of time in France, where his daughter is at school. She was with him on that day, and so were a nephew and a niece from the United States who happened to be in Europe at the time. Also traveling with them was a young dog, really a puppy, which Scott had acquired in southern France. He was driving a very old car loaned to him by a friend who lived in the vicinity. It was a noisy and unreliable vehicle.

I heard afterward that just as this group arrived in the suburb of Paris where the top-secret Lindbergh Families meeting was to take place, the muffler fell off the car. The vehicle then made such a racket that all the French housewives in the neighborhood came running out onto their lawns to see what was going on.

During the gathering itself, a casual picnic behind a suburban home, the puppy got tangled in its leash under the table, and had to be rescued by the children. It was a very successful occasion.

How do I fold this story into my memories of my father, with the familiar sights and sounds and smells: his gray fedora, his tan manila envelopes, the voice he used to call the children? Do I put it away in his closet, along with his traveling briefcase and the clean and distant official scent of the military uniform that hung there, mixed with the pungent odor of well-shined shoes?

Some of my family memories are as bright and clear as ever in my mind: memories of listening to the stories my father told by the fireplace in the old house in Connecticut; memories of taking walks in the woods with him and trying to keep up with his long strides, he wearing his navy blue jacket and sometimes that funny-looking fur hat he had, with the earflaps; memories of learning to swim by hanging on tight to his shoulders as he swam out of our little cove toward Long Island Sound in his powerful, even breast-stroke, his large hands parting the phosphorescence before us in the darkness of an August night.

But I certainly could have done without his endless lectures on the Population Explosion, with all those graphs and charts on "exponential growth curves" (that's a direct quote). How could he have done this with a straight face, let alone a clear conscience? A man who fathered thirteen—I think, I still have to stop and count us!—children, haranguing one of his daughters about world population figures? Give me a break!

And every time I think about that awful letter my sister kept locked away for all those years, I get mad all over again.

It helps to hear from the humorists: "Gee, this will come in handy if any of you needs an extra kidney!" There are other comforts, too.

It is very interesting, in an odd way, to have one's ideas about the structure of the personal world change so rapidly, especially at my age. I am watching so many of my long-held assumptions dissolve into a new reality, like dreams in daylight: the assumption that my parents had a complex but traditionally "faithful" marriage; the assumption that my father always wandered the world alone and unloved, a kind of roving monk, until he came home to us; the assumption that my father was by his very nature unable to deceive. I didn't believe his theories and I never paid full attention to his lectures, but I always thought of my father as a kind of Scandinavian-American George Washington, someone who could not tell, or live, a lie.

Mine is not as unique an experience as I had thought it was, and that is interesting, too. Since I first learned about my new brothers and sisters, several people have come to me with similar stories. One man learned in middle age that he had an uncle he had never known about. A woman met not one, or two, but five of her father's former mistresses at his funeral. Another woman, with several siblings, was a member of her father's "secret family," and was treated with rudeness and hostility by the "legitimate" family on the one occasion when they met. She said it was a terrible moment in her life.

I also saw the film *My Architect,* in which Louis Kahn's son Nathaniel searches for the truth about his own famous father, a man who also had several families. The film was well done and quite touching, I thought, but it left me dissatisfied and, again, annoyed with a man who could treat women and children this way, however great his "genius." It seemed a double injustice that the child of such a man first suffered the secrecies and constant absences of the father, then the imposition of a mythic paternal presence after the father died. My sense after watching the film was that children of such fathers, even if they barely knew them, may never be free of them.

There does not appear to be a prescribed etiquette for how the families treat one another, so I suppose we each make up our own or follow the one we learned. My mother taught me, mainly by example, that there is no circumstance in life that excuses bad manners.

She died two years before the news about the other families was revealed, and I have wondered how much she knew about my father's secret life. A close friend of hers told me this: "She knew, but she didn't know *what* she knew . . ." That sounds very like my mother. I have remembered in recent months that my parents, who may not have been lifelong lovers, shared a remarkably strong bond and were certainly lifelong friends and partners. I witnessed that partnership over many years.

A year after Scott's meeting with them, I took a trip to Europe to meet my half brothers and sisters. These newly discovered siblings were very gracious when I proposed to visit them, and I have learned through many years of experience that when a piece of upsetting news comes roaring out of my "Lindbergh" history to threaten the quiet life I love, the best corrective action, for me, is always personal connection.

When I meet and talk with people directly, sharing meals with them, taking walks in their neighborhoods, playing with their children, I cannot at the same time maintain a sense of sensationalism and scandal in my mind, or take refuge in self-indulgent melodrama. I dislike melodrama anyway, even in situations that seem to cry out for hair tearing, breast-beating, and rending of garments. I don't have the soul for it, or even the garments. I'd rather spend my time making friends.

Not wanting to impose myself upon my relatives too intimately or for too long, I arranged hotel reservations in the various locations ahead of my arrival, with their help. I planned my travel schedule to permit only a day, or two days at most, in each place.

It was clear from the yearlong correspondence before our meeting that there was no lack of goodwill between the American and European relatives, but I wondered about the tone our meetings would take. Would we feel joyful or serious as we acknowledged our odd parental connection for the first time face-to-face? Would we express anger together about our shared father, or would we talk of our compassion for him, and our love for our mothers? Was there a place for sadness? Embarrassment? What was the essential nature of our relationship, what was its quality? Was a secret, international collection of half siblings a sacred entity, or was the whole thing just a bit ridiculous?

After thinking myself into tighter and tighter circles with such questions, I concluded they didn't help me at all. The only reasonable thing for me to do was to travel to Europe without preconception or rehearsal, bringing a few gifts and some photos of my family and the farm, and hoping for the best.

That trip to Europe offered a mixture of experiences and emotions. I traveled for about ten days, mostly by train, and visited one relative after another. It was, at times, like traveling in a dream. I had not been to Europe for many years so I was already disoriented by the changes that had taken place since my last visit. It was hard to get used to paying my way with euros in every country, rather than changing money at each border and using local currency. The money seemed too easy to use, as if created for a twenty-first-century theme park called "Europe" rather than the coin of a real continent with distinct countries immersed over the centuries in their own traditions.

There were so few limits left, I thought as I traveled, so few separations between one thing and another. Nobody asked to see my passport when the train crossed the border between Germany and Switzerland, or when I took the TGV, the high-speed train from Lausanne to Paris. At the border between Switzerland and

France I expected to see a French gendarme, perhaps with a mustache and a handsome dark blue uniform, like Claude Rains in *Casablanca*. The train never even stopped. It kept on moving past Geneva and onward to Paris without even a pause, dissolving the boundaries I had known as a child and melting old barriers as if they had never existed. There seemed to be nothing at all to obstruct passage between Lucerne and Paris, between Berlin and Munich, and Connecticut and Vermont.

The European landscape, at least, was familiar. Riding through the countryside of western Europe on a train today, even in the presence of new technologies and modern cities, still gives a feeling of what that part of the world has been like for the last three hundred years. Little towns, prosperous-looking farms, clusters of houses with red-tiled roofs, fields of wheat and fields of poppies, all of these went by my window. I was glad to see them. On one leg of my trip, in Switzerland, my train rolled along the shores of Lac Léman near Vevey, the town where I lived with my mother and father the year I was fifteen. From my perspective it all looked exactly as it had forty-odd years ago. Was I asleep or was I awake? What year was this?

In 1960, most of my family lived in Europe. Two of my brothers were grown and married with families of their own in the United States, but my sister was studying in Paris, my brother Scott boarded at the International School in Geneva, and I attended St. George's School for Girls, a British school located in the tiny community of La-Tour-de-Peilz, not far from the apartment my parents had rented near Vevey. Every weekday morning I'd walk down the hill and get on a blue-and-white Swiss bus that made its way along the road by the lake and deposited me and another St. George's day student at a bus stop in the town of Clarens. From there we walked up another hill to the school. I wore an ugly school uniform, studied French, German, European history, and what the British students called "maths," and made friends with girls from Greece and India and Pakistan and Africa.

Though the school admitted students of different faiths from all over the world, we had morning prayers every day, and these were unmistakably Christian. One of my best friends, also a day student, was an American Quaker from Connecticut with an independent spirit. She got into trouble with our thin and daunting headmistress right away because she refused to kneel in prayer during the prayer service. Instead she sat quietly through the program, the way the non-Christian students did, with her legs crossed. The school authorities were very upset, especially when my friend reasonably pointed out that had the school authorities themselves been kneeling to pray, they would not have noticed.

Following much discussion with my friend and further discussion with my friend's mother, the headmistress capitulated. She said that if this student really wanted to sit cross-legged during morning prayers, she was welcome to go ahead and do so, "with the heathen."

My friend and I were shocked to the depths of our New England souls by these words. The headmistress was referring to our non-Christian classmates and friends, among them a Muslim princess from India, a Turkish girl who spoke four languages, and the daughter of the Oxford-educated president of Liberia.

As my train continued along the lake toward Lausanne, I remembered the friends with whom I'd spent that brief, happy, irreverent international year. I felt thoroughly warmed by affection and nostalgia, though I was well aware that my fifteen-year-old self and her cohorts from around the globe would have laughed mercilessly at the lump in my throat.

On the journey to meet my father's other children, it was my half siblings themselves who gave me the most assistance, and I needed every bit of it. I have been absentminded all my life, and I get lost easily everywhere. I always find myself again, so this doesn't worry me too much, but it can be of concern to my family. A niece and her husband bought me a cell phone for Europe, and early in my train travels one of my half sisters loaned me another, which she called a "handy." These phones both looked to me very much like the cell phone I travel with at home, but I never figured out how to use either one of them. Luckily, by some miracle, I didn't get lost once.

Because people were taking such good care of me, I'd get to the station well ahead of my scheduled departure time, and could count on one of my new relatives to be waiting at the station at the other end. Interestingly, it never took more than a few seconds for us to recognize each other at the station. I suspect this was due less to family resemblance than to the fact that we were looking for each other so intently. If you are trying to catch your first glimpse of a brother you have never seen before, you look harder.

My two sisters and five brothers took very good care of me. I am most grateful to them, and I feel very protective of them. I had never been an older sister before.

They were all quite solicitous of their much older sister traveling all by herself. I smiled when I overheard one of them talking to another on the phone just before taking me to the train station: "I'll put her on the train here at 10:00 A.M. You'll pick her up on your end at 3:00 P.M. right?" This was exactly the way my sister and I used to talk about my mother in her later years: *I'll drive her north as far as Greenfield, Mass. You meet me at the Howard Johnson's there, and take her the rest of the way to Vermont, okay?*

Every stop on my journey was different in feeling. There were cheerful visits in city cafés and there were long walks and serious talks deep in the countryside. There was a noisy afternoon barbecue in a family backyard, and a quiet visit in the suburban living room of a house where a baby was due any minute.

There were some lovely encounters with children. I went to one child's riding lesson, took a long walk in the woods to identify mushrooms with two others, pored over a wedding album with a fourth and learned the names of the bride's godmother and the groom's best man. I sat in a tent with yet another child, who giggled over my dismal failure to assemble a puzzle-map of France.

None of the children seemed particularly interested in their ancestors or in the intricacies of our relationships, but everybody loved my photographs of the sheep and of the fish Nat and Ben had caught in our pond.

Every so often the oddness of it all came through. Once, during a meal, a European half brother and I looked at each other and slowly shook our heads, wordless. *This is absolutely normal and completely insane, too.* Another time, during a sunny, happy meal outdoors by a lake in Germany with a group of friends and relatives, a handsome older gentleman in the group asked me politely in perfect English, "Tell me, Reeve, how many brothers and sisters do you have?" It was a reasonable question for normal circumstances, but the whole table went silent as we took in the full implication of what he had asked. Then, thank goodness, we all burst out laughing.

My favorite memory is of the moment toward the end of my trip when I met the final brother in my European family. He was and is a delightful man, and he walked through the doorway of the house where I was staying with a twinkle in his eye and said, "Here I am, Reeve—the last Goldberg Variation!"

I don't like telling other people's secrets if they don't want them told, and in my family it is hard to be sure. Some of my American family members and some of my European brothers and sisters are outgoing, "public" personalities. They resent the confining darkness of old secrets and old scandals, and they desperately seek the light. One or two may periodically seek the limelight, too, exploring the publicity that has been associated with the Lindbergh name since 1927, for better and for worse. These family members give interviews, participate in television documentaries, offer comments to the press. They may publish books about their lives and their thoughts, just as I do. If criticized, they ask why they should not be free to celebrate their heritage, the way others in the family have done. Why should they not tell the truth, as they know it, to their children, to the public, to the world?

I understand their point of view. Not only that, but as one who has given interviews, written books, and celebrated Lindbergh heritage in a public way, I am in no position to criticize anybody else who does the same thing.

There are other family members, though, who are very private by nature. They recoil from publicity. They don't want to write books and give interviews, or to be included in such things in any way. They feel deeply betrayed and damaged by the revelations of personal and family secrets. After all, the family story is their story, too, and if they had a choice, they would prefer that it be kept private. They are horrified to have had their personal business aired in public. Some are deeply distressed on behalf of their still-living mothers, who have kept their secrets for fifty years and had hoped to end their lives in privacy and in peace. Instead, these women have been devastated by exposure. Their secrets have been revealed, their privacy has been invaded, and their personal information has been spread over the tabloid news on two continents. I can understand this point of view just as well.

On one train, traveling between cities and families in Europe, I wrote this in my journal:

These are good, intelligent, warmhearted, and thoughtful people, their childhoods and upbringing very similar to mine. There is independence of spirit and a quiet style of life . . . The great gap, the divide and chasm I perceive, has to do with the breach of privacy in the revelation of the family secret. For some it is like a matter of breaking out from underground . . . for others it is like having not only your protective clothing but also your very skin and flesh torn away, leaving raw tissue, bleeding, and pain.

This language may seem a bit extreme coming from someone who claims to dislike melodrama, but being in my family is like a melodrama sometimes, with a story line that is simultaneously powerfully compelling and utterly baffling.

I have no conclusions to draw and no explanations to give, but about a month after I returned home from Europe, I dreamed about my father. This is what I wrote in my journal when I woke up the next morning:

August 4, 2004 . . . quickly, before it goes, I had a dream about my father last night, for the first time I can remember, in years—he was just there, wherever I was, looking as he always did, only his hair a little messy—that one long silver lock that he combed over his bald spot, normally, now falling over his forehead—he was standing, and shifting his weight a bit, maybe poised for flight? He did not seem troubled when I explained without speaking, as one does in dreams, that I'd spent time with the European children. He seemed . . . affirmative . . . Oh, yes, that's right, uh-huh, they're good people, I'm glad you think so . . . no anger, just a kind of quiet satisfaction. But when I ventured the thought that his children had been hurt by all of this, all his children, there was nothing. He just didn't get it.

I still remember the feeling I had about the dream when I woke up. At that moment I thought I knew the truth about my father. I thought I knew with absolute certainty that the problem was not that my father wasn't willing to listen to what I was saying to him, the part about causing pain to his children. The problem was that he literally could not hear the message. With all his gifts and his abilities, he had come into the world without one very specific piece of listening equipment, and whatever it was, it was critical to a complete understanding of the sufferings of other people. Until the dream lost its hold and I came fully awake, I was sure I had the answer.

My father died in August 1974, just a month before I turned twenty-nine years old. I was pregnant with my younger daughter, Susannah, at the time. When she was born a few months later, I cried because I noticed that she had a dimple in her chin, just like my father's. I thought of the dimple as a gift from the grandfather she would never meet. I missed him enormously, intimately, personally, with his presence sharp and dear to me, my grief intermingling with my joy, that day. I still miss him, sometimes, and still remember him in detail, but the detail is less sharp now. Of all the people I have known and loved, my father is the one I found most impenetrable.

I have the feeling that he was the only person involved with all these families who knew the full truth, and I keep thinking that by the time he died in 1974, my father had made his life so complicated that he had to keep each part separate from the other parts, the way a finicky child will divide the food on a dinner plate so the meat loaf never comes into contact with the carrots or the mashed potatoes. I don't know why he lived this way, and I don't think I ever will know, but what it means to me is that every intimate human connection my father had during his later years was fractured by secrecy. He could not be completely open with anybody who loved him anywhere on earth. Now that the sensationalism has diminished and my own emotions have calmed down, what remains with me is a sense of his unutterable loneliness.

Last summer my sister from Paris and her four children came to stay with us. They speak French and German and a little English, too. We spent a couple of weeks together in Vermont, swimming in the pond and sightseeing in town and wandering around the countryside. One night my niece and her mother and I went with some friends to see *The Devil Wears Prada*. We admired Meryl Streep in three languages and we ate much too much buttered popcorn.

Another day Nat showed the three nephews how to fish for trout, and the two younger boys caught a beautiful rainbow. The two younger boys are not very big but they insisted on reeling in the fish themselves anyway, the two of them, with exclamations and struggles over who would hold the rod. *"Laisse-moi!"* ("Let me do it!").

Their older brother caught a fish, too, a smaller brook trout. We took pictures of both fish, and everybody politely admired everybody else's fishing skills, but I could hear one of my small nephews whispering to the other, *"Le notre est plus bel . . ."* ("Ours is prettier").

Toward the end of their visit, I looked out my kitchen window one afternoon and saw these same little boys running through the hayfield with a couple of balsa wood airplanes, the kind my children used to play with. We played with them, too, when I was a child. They come unassembled in a clear bag with instructions and all the parts precut, ready to be punched out and put together so the plane can be launched into the sky.

These planes are delicate, so they don't last too long, but they are beautiful in the air. I watched as the two children ran together and threw the airplanes as high as they could to float over the farm and dive lightly and fall into the grass where they could find them and throw them again, and again, and yet again. They called back and forth to each other: something about the airplanes, something about the wind, something about the day. I couldn't hear them, and if I could I might not have understood what they were saying in the childhood language of another country. All the same, I kept on watching.

I am not the oldest unwed mother in Caledonia County anymore, and I'm not sure that I ever really deserved that title, much as I loved it. It was helpful to me at the time. There have been other times in my life when I felt the need to title and describe myself, perhaps so I would understand a little better who I was and what I was doing, what I was useful for in the world: "daughter of"; "sister of"; "wife of"; "mother of"; "teacher of"; "writer of." It is good to have a description handy, and I've appreciated the ones available to me. My sister, Anne, has gone, but it is comforting to know I have sisters, still, and lately I've been happy to realize that it is time to add "Grandmother of" to all the other descriptions.

I'm hoping that as I get older I'll get braver, and someday I may even be brave enough to leave some of my old descriptions and preoccupations behind me, to let the family history go, let it be. Gently, so as not to disturb anybody, I may open a door and just walk through it. I may tiptoe away from the closed rooms of the past with all their stories, and move quietly into the present I love so well, and then even further, out into the open future, forward from here.

Reading List

These are books I was reading or thinking about while I was writing this book.

Adamson, Joy. *Born Free: A Lioness of Two Worlds.* New York: Vintage, 1974.

Angelou, Maya. *Even the Stars Look Lonesome.* New York: Random House, 1997.

Boni, Margaret Bradford. *Fireside Book of Folk Songs.* New York: Simon and Schuster, 1947.

Brown, Dan. *Angels & Demons.* New York: Pocket Books, 2006.

———. *The Da Vinci Code.* New York: Doubleday, 2004.

Cheever, Susan. *Note Found in a Bottle: My Life as a Drinker: A Memoir.* New York: Simon & Schuster, 1999.

Cobb, Boughton. *A Field Guide to the Ferns and Their Related Families.* Boston: Houghton Mifflin, 1963.

Conant, Roger. *A Field Guide to Reptiles and Amphibians of the United States and Canada East of the 100th Meridian.* Boston: Houghton Mifflin, 1958.

Craniotomy: Understanding Your Care from Start to Finish. Prepared by the Nurses on the Neuroscience Unit, Dartmouth-Hitchcock Medical Center, Lebanon, NH.

Desai, Kiran. *The Inheritance of Loss.* New York: Atlantic Monthly Press, 2006.

Reading List

Dinesen, Isak. *Out of Africa.* London: Putnam, 1946.

Flaubert, Gustave. *Madame Bovary.* New York: Barnes & Noble Classics, 2005.

García Márquez, Gabriel. *One Hundred Years of Solitude.* Trans. by Gregory Rabassa. New York: Harper & Row, 1970.

Gasztold, Carmen Bernos de. *Prayers from the Ark.* Trans. by Rumer Godden. New York: Viking Press, 1962.

Goldberg, Natalie. *Writing Down the Bones: Freeing the Writer Within.* Boston: Shambhala, 2005.

Grumbach, Doris. *Extra Innings: A Memoir.* New York: W. W. Norton, 1993.

Kinnell, Galway. *Mortal Acts, Mortal Words.* Boston: Houghton Mifflin, 1980.

Klotz, Alexander. *A Field Guide to the Butterflies of North America, East of the Great Plains.* Boston: Houghton Mifflin, 1951.

Lawrence, D. H. *Lady Chatterley's Lover.* Boston: G. K. Hall, 1993.

Lindbergh, Anne Morrow. *Gift from the Sea.* New York: Pantheon, 1955.

———. *The Unicorn and Other Poems, 1935–1955.* New York: Pantheon, 1956.

Lindbergh, Reeve, and Kathryn Brown. *Grandmother.* Cambridge, MA: Candlewick Press, 2007.

Ludlum, David M. *The Audubon Society Field Guide to North American Weather.* New York: Alfred A. Knopf, 1991.

Metalious, Grace. *Peyton Place.* New York: Messner, 1956.

Mosher, Howard Frank. *On Kingdom Mountain.* Boston: Houghton Mifflin, 2007.

Nafisi, Azar. *Reading Lolita in Tehran: A Memoir in Books.* New York: Random House 2003.

Paley, Grace. "On Mother's Day," in *Begin Again: Collected Poems.* New York: Farrar, Straus, & Giroux, 2000.

Perrin, Noel. *First Person Rural: Essays of a Sometime Farmer.* New York: Penguin, 1980.

———. *Solo: Life with an Electric Car.* New York: W. W. Norton, 1992.

Peterson, Lee. *A Field Guide to Edible Wild Plants of Eastern and Central North America.* Boston: Houghton Mifflin, 1978.

Reading List

Peterson, Roger Tory. *A Field Guide to the Birds,* Second Revised and Enlarged Edition. (Sponsored by the National Audubon Society.) Boston: Houghton Mifflin, 1947.

Rehder, Harold A. *National Audubon Society Field Guide to North American Seashells.* New York: Alfred A. Knopf, 2003.

Stevens, Wallace. *Poems.* New York: Vintage Books, 1959.

Strunk, William, Jr., and E. B. White. *The Elements of Style.* New York: Macmillan, 1957.

Toklas, Alice B. *The Alice B. Toklas Cookbook.* New York: Harper & Brothers, 1954 (Anchor Books, 1960).

Trollope, Anthony. *Barchester Towers.* New York: Alfred A. Knopf, 1992.

———. *Rachel Ray.* New York: Dover, 1980.

———. *Sir Harry Hotspur of Humblethwaite.* New York: Dover, 1985.

———. *The Vicar of Bullhampton.* New York: Oxford University Press, 1990.

Watts, Alan. *The Way of Zen.* New York: Pantheon, 1957.

White, E. B. *Stuart Little.* New York: Harper & Row, 1973.

Zinsser, William. *On Writing Well: The Classic Guide to Writing Nonfiction.* New York: Harper Perennial, 2004.

Acknowledgments

It is impossible to thank every single person who helps to bring a book into being, because so many contributions and influences are invisible even to the author. Still, I want to say how grateful I am to my friends and beloved family members all over the world, especially my three "Brothers Grim," Jon, Land, and Scott, and their families, and my late sister, Anne. She was with me, I am absolutely sure, every step of the way.

Thanks to my wonderful agent, Jennie Dunham, to her assistants, Melanie Klesse and Blair Hewes, and to Bob Bender, Johanna Li, Gypsy da Silva, and those at Simon & Schuster whose patience, encouragement, and gentle expertise have once again moved me along from vague notions to finished proofs. I don't know how you do it, but I'm very glad you did.

Here in Vermont, I am grateful to the End-of-the-Road Writers and the Reading Group, to the staff and board of the St. Johnsbury Athenaeum, and to the Tennis Ladies, for nourishment of every kind. Thanks to Robin Berenbaum and Sharon Biddle, to Gretchen and Duncan Bond, to Carol and Patton Hyman, and to Catherine Thomas for steadfast friendship, day by day and week by week, no matter how crazy things got—and they did.

Finally, my family: Nat Tripp, Alice Wardwell Tripp, Connie Feydy, Lizzy and Dave Lindenberg, Eli and Kara Tripp (and Phoebe and Stetson!), Susannah and Jon Scanlon, Marek Sapieyevski, Sam

Acknowledgments

Tripp, and Ben Tripp. I don't think I can even begin to say how grateful I am to you, individually and together, not only for the support you have given but also for the great gift of being in my life. (And for understanding about turtles.)